MW00560246

Chesed Shel Emet
The Truest Act of Kindness
Exploring the Meaning of Taharah

An Expanded Third Edition

Chesed Shel Emet
The Truest Act of Kindness
Exploring the Meaning of Taharah

An Expanded Third Edition

✧

Rabbi Stuart Kelman
Dan Fendel

EKS Publishing Co., Oakland, California

First Edition Project Editor
Jessica W. Goldstein

Third Edition Book Design
Inna Inker Goldshteyn

First Edition Book Design
Irene Imfeld

Chesed Shel Emet: The Truest Act of Kindness, Third Edition,
© 2013 by Rabbi Stuart Kelman and Dan Fendel. Printed in the United
States. No part of this book may be transmitted or reproduced by any
means, electronic or mechanical, without written permission, except for
brief quotations included in critical articles and reviews. For information
contact the publisher.

Ronna Kabatznick's article originally appeared as "Preparing the
Dead for Life's Final Passage" in *The Forward*. It is reprinted here with the
permission of *The Forward*.

EKS Publishing Co.
P.O. Box 9750
Berkeley, CA 94709-0750
e-mail: orders@ekspublishing.com

Phone (510) 251-9100, Fax (510) 251-9102
www.ekspublishing.com

Second Printing, March 2014
ISBN 978-0-939144-71-6

An Introductory Prayer
Before Performing a Taharah

Source of kindness and compassion, whose ways are ways of mercy and truth, You have commanded us to act with loving kindness and righteousness toward the dead, and to engage in their proper burial. Grant us the courage and the strength to properly perform this work, this holy task of cleaning and washing the body, dressing the dead in shrouds, and burying the deceased. Forgive us for any errors we may commit during the process. Guide our hands and hearts as we do this work, and enable us to fulfill the commandment of love. Help us see Your face in the face of the deceased, even as we see You in the faces of those who share this task with us. Source of life and death, be with us now and always.

Reprinted with permission from *PSJC Hevra Kadisha Taharah Manual*, 2nd ed. (Brooklyn, NY: Park Slope Jewish Center, 2009).

Contents

Foreword to the Expanded Third Edition

"The highest act of *gemilut chesed* (acts of loving kindness) is that which is done for the dead, for there can never be any thought of repayment."
TANCHUMA VAYECHI 107A

This statement, found in a late Byzantine-era homiletical Midrash, first published in 1522, shapes Judaism's view of how to care for and give respect to the body from the time of death until burial. This care consists of two parts: watching or guarding the body (*shmirah*) and physical preparation of the body (*taharah**). This second part, which entails the preparation of the body for burial, consists of five stages: Opening prayers (including *mechilah*—asking forgiveness from the deceased); *rechitzah* (physical washing of the body); *taharah* (ritual washing of the body); *halbashah* (dressing the body) together with *halanah* (placing the body in the *aron* [casket]); and concluding prayers.

There is no *mitzvah* more important than this one. Preparing the body for its final journey takes precedence over all other commandments because burial needs to be completed as soon as possible after death. The importance of *taharah* is grounded in Judaism's understanding of the immutable nature of *kedushah* (sanctity). Judaism holds that the body is a holy receptacle into which God places the soul, and that holy vessels retain their essential holiness even when the physical structure is damaged or destroyed. *Gesher Hachayim*, a treatise on life by Harav Yechiel Michel Tucazinsky (1949), compares the human to a living Torah scroll. Just as a Torah scroll remains holy after it can no longer be used, the human body remains holy even after death. Indeed, we often use the term *met/metah* ("deceased") rather than "body" to emphasize our awareness that we are dealing with the physical manifestation of a human being with a soul. In keeping with these beliefs, great care and respect are accorded to the body as it is prepared for burial and escorted to the cemetery. The most fundamental principle underlying this work is *k'vod hamet* (respect for the dead), and this rabbinic principle governs the decision-making at each step in the process. For instance, we do not carry on idle conversation during

---

*The term *taharah* refers to the whole second part of the care, to a particular act within or section of this second part, and to a level of personal status. As a personal status, the term is often translated as "ritual purity" but see our discussion under "*Tahor* and *Tamei*" in the section "Five Underlying Concepts and Settings for *Taharah*" in Chapter 1.

the preparation of the body, and we keep the body covered at all times except when it is absolutely necessary to expose it.

In Judaism, water is often used as a transformative medium. Use of a *mikveh* and the act of *taharah* are two rituals that use water to mark one's transition from one state to another. Before marriage, for example, we immerse ourselves in the *mikveh* because we are about to change our status. During the *process* of *taharah*, water is poured over the body to prepare it for burial and elevate it from the ordinary to a higher plane of holiness.

The *mitzvah* of *taharah* is so important that those who volunteer for the task of preparing the *met/metah* are formally organized into a group called a *Chevra Kadisha,* or Holy Society. The *Chevra Kadisha* clearly originated in Talmudic times (see *Mo'ed Katan* 27b), and was so central to Jewish life that whenever a new community took root, this Holy Society was one of the first groups established.

This manual contains procedures and prayers based on traditional sources, and we acknowledge that some of the prayers may not be consistent with an individual's own personal theology (see the new Preface for this Edition). A pervasive theme of *taharah* is the notion that the *neshamah* (soul) is moving on to another stage, and that the nature of this transition is affected by one's moral and religious behavior: that is, good behavior is rewarded, and bad behavior is punished. While many of us might prefer to temper this view of a direct and causal relationship, we would strongly encourage the recitation of the prayers as they appear because they are ancient and they have maintained an emotional hold over our people for generations. These prayers continue to remind us that all of life is ultimately in God's hands. The *taharah* prayers help us regain our balance in this world, a balance that is necessary to perform this *mitzvah* of *chesed shel emet,* the truest act of kindness.

Why a New Edition?

This manual was written originally for members of Congregation Netivot Shalom's *Chevra Kadisha* so that they would have a printed guide to consult before, during, and after they engage in this important *mitzvah*. In 2010, Kavod v'Nichum, an international organization of individuals, groups, and organizations such as synagogues involved in *Chevra Kadisha* work, launched an on-line program of study called the Gamliel Institute. This Institute is designed to train leaders throughout the world who would work towards reclaiming the *mitzvot* of *k'vod hamet* and *nichum aveilim* (comforting of mourners). One of the Institute's five academic courses focuses on *taharah* and *shmirah,* and therefore concerns itself with the specifics of the *taharah* ritual.

In putting together the earlier editions of this manual as a how-to document for *taharah,* it seemed sufficient to simply *present* the traditional prayers, which are primarily a collection of Biblical verses. But often, when the liturgy is recited by the *m'taharim* (those who perform the *taharah* ritual), the words are said perfunctorily, if at all; sometimes in English, usually mumbled in Hebrew. For the purpose of the Gamliel course on *taharah,* co-teachers David Zinner (Executive Director of Kavod v'Nichum) and Rabbi Stuart Kelman wanted to look deeper. They wanted Gamliel students to be able to take the recitation to a higher level, and realized that this would be enhanced by studying the prayers from the perspective of the discipline of liturgy. To their knowledge, this had never been done before (perhaps because the *taharah* ritual has long been practiced somewhat in secrecy).

As the course unfolded, one of the students, Dan Fendel, took a strong interest in this liturgical analysis, and over the next year or so, he and Rabbi Kelman wrote a paper on the subject. This work led to a recognition of how the liturgy gives an insight into Jewish theology as well as into how we care for the body of the *met/metah.* The goal of the paper was to unpack the prayers, by understanding how they work and how they function. The paper did not try to present a critical interpretation of the prayers, nor a historical review of their development, and certainly not a kabbalistic underpinning of each section (which is absolutely needed for a complete understanding), but simply to respond to and understand their usage and meaning in the *taharah* room itself.

In creating this new edition of *Chesed Shel Emet,* we have collaborated to embed the ideas of the paper into the earlier version of the manual. This edition still contains the practical steps to be taken during *taharah,* but now includes a deeper understanding of the workings of the ritual. Our intent is to unravel the mysteries of *taharah* and apply the principles of liturgical analysis to help show the beauty of these words and actions. Along the way, we have re-examined the choices and organization of the liturgy, reviewed and revised the translations, and corrected an assortment of errors. Biblical translations in this work are based on the 1985 translation of the Jewish Publication Society. Talmudic translations are based on the ArtScroll edition of the Babylonian Talmud. Translations from *Ma'avar Yabok* are from the work of Rabbi Dr. Steven A. Moss. Other translations are our own.

Transliterations are also our own. Our goal with transliteration (and with capitalization) has been consistency of style, though we make occasional exceptions for familiar terms. Transliterations of Hebrew words are generally italicized. Punctuation has been included in verses from *Tanach* where it seemed necessary in order to clarify the meaning for the reader.

Acknowledgments

We both acknowledge with heartfelt appreciation our friend, colleague, and publisher, Claudia Valas at EKS Publishing. Throughout this process, she has encouraged us and guided us through the necessary steps to publication. And to Samuel J. Salkin, Executive Director of Sinai Memorial Chapel Chevra Kadisha in San Francisco goes our profound gratitude. As both a friend and a student when this new material was presented, Sam was so taken with the *mitzvah* of getting this new material into the hands of you, the reader, that he committed to raising the necessary resources. Sinai Memorial Chapel Chevra Kadisha and the authors are deeply appreciative of the generosity of the Milton and Sophie Meyer Fund for its generosity in supporting this publication.

We want to thank our four outside readers—Rabbi Edward Feld (Senior Editor, *Mahzor Lev Shalem*), Rabbi Richard Sarason (Professor of Rabbinic Literature and Thought, Hebrew Union College—Jewish Institute of Religion), Jacob Z. Stromer (Teaneck, New Jersey), and Henry Wulf (*Chevra Kadisha*, Congregation Olam Tikvah, Fairfax, Virginia)—as well as David Zinner, for their excellent and substantive comments on the manuscript. This book has benefited from their insights. And finally, our thanks to Kavod v'Nichum and the Gamliel Institute, as well as to all of the Gamliel students and the participants at Kavod v'Nichum conferences who studied with us, corrected our errors, made major comments and additions, and thus enabled us to reach this day.

We wish to dedicate this volume to David Zinner, the "godfather" of this new and invigorated movement of *Chevra Kadisha* workers. We have often joked that we need to clone David so that everyone can share of his wisdom. This book marks, in small measure, our way of doing just that.

Rabbi Stuart Kelman
Dan Fendel
Gamliel Institute
Pesach 5773

For more information about the Gamliel Institute, see www.jewish-funerals.org.

Foreword to the Second Edition

Since the publication of the first edition of this booklet, many other manuals have appeared, many of which are listed in the updated bibliography. This fact alone attests to both the increasing prominence of this *mitzvah* in the consciousness and practices of North American Jewry and the desire to return the practice of *taharah* to its prior location, the synagogue and the local community.

The major changes in this edition, apart from clarifying instructions, for which I am indebted to the members of the Congregation Netivot Shalom *Chevra Kadisha*, are the inclusion of a *mechilah*, 'request for forgiveness' paragraph before the *taharah*, and an updated bibliography.

In the first edition, I inadvertently omitted to acknowledge Dr. Debbie Findling as a major contributor. In that spirit, I wish to give her special recognition to indicate the vast amount of work she did in its creation. As well, our publisher, Claudia Valas at EKS Publishing, has provided both tangible and intangible support so that we might make the work of a *Chevra Kadisha* more public and pronounced. Over the years, I have also benefited greatly from the advice and wisdom of David Zinner, my friend, and executive director of Kavod v'Nichum (Honor and Comfort), which provides assistance, training and resources about death and bereavement practice for *Chevra Kadisha* groups in synagogues and communities throughout the U.S. and Canada. I, and everyone associated with the rise in stature and consciousness of the work of the many individuals and *Chevrei Kadisha* in North America, are deeply indebted to David's vision and passion. I invite you to simply look at the website www.jewish-funerals.org to gain an insight into his many accomplishments.

This work is indeed *avodat hakodesh*, holy work, and I feel truly blessed to be able to make a small contribution to furthering the performance of this *mitzvah*.

Rabbi Stuart Kelman
Founding Rabbi
Congregation Netivot Shalom
Berkeley, CA
Pesach 5768

Foreword to the First Edition

Laws of *taharah* have deep historical roots. Beginning in Mishnaic times, specific procedures and customs evolved in a variety of locations and through many generations. As a result, numerous traditions exist today. This booklet needs to be seen in that light: It is one link in the great chain of our Jewish tradition.

The *Chevra Kadisha* at Congregation Netivot Shalom came into being in 1990, just one year after our synagogue's founding. It was a response to immediate needs as we found ourselves facing the deaths of congregants and their family members. In Berkeley, there was no Jewish funeral home on which to rely, so we began by apprenticing ourselves to the Orthodox *Chevra Kadisha* at Congregation Beth Jacob in Oakland, California. After three years of training, we felt competent to perform our own *taharot*. We also felt that the booklet used by Beth Jacob's *Chevra Kadisha* was not well suited to our Conservative congregation. This volume is the result of our efforts to create *taharah* guidelines appropriate for a variety of denominations.

Our procedures and readings are adapted from the following sources: *Regulations and Procedure including Traditional Prayers and Translations for the Jewish Sacred Society*; *Procedures for the Chevra Kadisha*; *A Selection of Verses for the Chevra Kadisha*; *The Jewish Way in Death and Mourning*; and *Tahara Guide Prepared for the New Haven Chevra Kadisha*. More information about each of these sources appears in the bibliography. Most of the prayers in this book are traditional verses. I have modernized the English translations, used gender-sensitive language, added transliterations of the Hebrew, and altered the Hebrew in a few places where it felt appropriate to do so.

I would like to thank Amy Bram, Jonathan Heinstein, Rachel Heinstein, Dr. Jo Milgrom, Chai Levy, and the many others who have contributed to this booklet. Netivot Shalom's *Chevra Kadisha* holds its annual meeting on or near the seventh of Adar (the date traditionally ascribed as the anniversary of Moses' death). At one time or another, members of that group have reviewed these materials, for which I thank them. May God bless all of these people, and all of you, with a long life and with blessings.

Rabbi Stuart Kelman
Congregation Netivot Shalom
Berkeley, CA
Rosh Hashanah 5761

Preface to the Expanded Third Edition

This Preface comes from Peter Strauss, who has done many taharot. His essay is a reflection about his experiences over many years. Peter is a member of Congregation Netivot Shalom in Berkeley.

What *Taharah* is Really About

Existentially we are preparing a body for burial. Nominally, we are doing *taharah* as a way of showing honor and respect to the deceased. It might be helpful to imagine that the body which we are manipulating is a living person, keeping in mind that one day, it will be us; this image may remind us to be as tender and careful in our ministrations as we would if it were so.

But there's more. We are told that the *neshamah*, the spirit of the deceased, is in the room with us. And while we're doing what resembles Zechariah's description of the preparation of the *Kohen Gadol* to enter the Holy of Holies, therein to meet the Divine, so that is what we're doing in relation to the *neshamah* of the deceased in front of us. We are, it can be said, preparing the deceased for two different destinations. On the one hand, we are preparing the physical part of the deceased for burial in the ground, from whence we all come. On the other hand, we are preparing the spiritual part, the *neshamah*, for an entrance into the presence of the Divine. It is essential that we keep both parts of the process in the front of our consciousness while we engage in the process of *taharah*. Our purpose is no less holy than the task that confronted those preparing the *Kohen Gadol*.

What we are doing is taking care of our own. Our way is special, and derives from the ancient traditions of our people. We are continuing that tradition, forging yet another link in the chain that binds us together, our ancestors, our descendants, and we ourselves. And while some others who deal with the bodies of the deceased might not have any spiritual dimension to their work, we most assuredly do. And that spiritual dimension is embodied in the liturgy of *taharah*.

Someone might well ask, "What if I don't believe this stuff? What if I'm really not sure how relevant any of this religious stuff is to me and my core beliefs?" I suggest that you Act As If it were all true. Another way of looking at what we're doing is as drama, as theater – we are the actors, the *met/metah* is an important but non-speaking part, and the *neshamah* and God are the audience. There are three entities in the *taharah* room: the team, the *neshamah*, and God. The conversations all take place between those three. And just as when we watch a play or a movie, we agree to believe that the actors are really the characters they represent, just as we agree to suspend disbelief so as to enter fully the action of the drama, so we need to suspend disbelief so as to enter fully into the drama that is *taharah*.

There are some who complain that the liturgical pieces of *taharah* interfere with doing the job at hand. On the other hand, it is quite possible to see the liturgy as what is in fact central, and being punctuated with the physical manipulations of the *met/metah*.

Why should we do this? Why should we set aside our own understandings and misgivings and beliefs or nonbeliefs to do *taharah* properly? Because we are not there to engage in our own theology. We are there on behalf of the deceased, and to assure his/her family and community that the deceased is being taken care of according to our traditions and practices. Since we are told that it was God who buried Moses, we are in that light also acting on behalf of God. And to Act As If the *neshamah* is right there, hovering over our shoulders, gives us a chance to do what we do soulfully and powerfully, and to focus on the objective: preparing for the meeting with the Divine. It is a powerful antidote to the morbid thoughts that might otherwise intrude when dealing with the physical reality of death. There will be plenty of time – the rest of your life, in fact – to deal with your own mortality. Doing *taharah* is not about you. It is about giving the greatest gift we have, our own spirituality, our own soulfulness, to the deceased before us. It might be as close as we can get, and live, to the face-to-face encounter with God.

Preface to the First Edition

The best possible introduction to taharah *is a first person account of the experience. Following are the thoughts of Ronna Kabatznick, originally published in* The Forward. *Ronna is a member of Congregation Netivot Shalom in Berkeley.*

The First Time

The three of us unwrapped her body and immediately covered it with a clean sheet. The dead woman looked to be in her late sixties. She was overweight, her hair gray and medium length. I was grateful that her eyes were shut. The solid, heavy body seemed frighteningly empty: no personality, no trace of movement. The team leader asked me to remove the woman's two identification tags—one from her wrist, the other from her ankle. I hesitated for a moment, took a deep breath, and, for the first time in my life, touched a dead human being.

Last winter I decided to become a member of the women's *taharah*, a division of the synagogue's burial society. *Taharah*—the ancient ritual of preparing bodies for burial—is the custom that marks the end of a Jew's life, just as circumcision or baby-naming marks the beginning. While most Jews are familiar with customs of mourning, *taharah* remains a mysterious rite performed by a few trained people, unobserved by family and friends. The chair of our burial society had put out a call for volunteers. Congregants at Netivot Shalom, a five-year-old Conservative synagogue in Berkeley, California, were quick to fill up the divisions concerned with the comfort of the living. They were, it seems, less enthusiastic about caring for the dead.

Like them, I initially recoiled: washing and preparing bodies evoke memories of childhood ghost stories, not feelings of compassion. But, on a recent Buddhist meditation retreat, I began to reexamine my feelings about death. I realized I could prepare the dead, and by doing so, I would be embracing life. I also hoped that a direct experience with death would make it seem less frightening and unnatural.

Soon after I volunteered, I received a call saying that someone in the Orthodox community had died, and they needed a third person for *taharah*. I was told to dress modestly and cover my head as a symbol of respect. Because there is no Jewish funeral home in our community, I was instructed to go to one in a seedy neighborhood in Oakland.

The team leader, Maya, an Israeli expert in halachic burial techniques, met me at the side door of the funeral home and introduced me to the third member of the team, an elderly Russian woman who spoke no English. We nodded to each other as Maya brought the necessary equipment. For the deceased: boards for elevating the body (it's considered disrespectful to turn the person over), buckets for washing, toothpicks for cleaning nails, bandages and tape to help cover wounds or sores, white linen shrouds, and earth from Israel. For the living: surgical gowns and gloves.

Nothing can really prepare you for seeing and touching a dead body. I had seen non-Jewish people after they died, made up and dressed at a funeral. It was nothing like the experience of being in the preparation room at a funeral home. After death, the body bloats and turns both cold and blue. Skin tears and bones break easily unless the body is handled with extreme care. The body is not only lifeless, but also vulnerable.

This booklet gives precise instructions for performing *taharah*. It is very exact and orderly, containing information including the following: unnecessary speech is prohibited; no part of the body is ever exposed unless it is washed; and team members must not turn their backs on the dead, because it is considered an expression of disrespect.

These delicate details support the basic functions of *taharah*: to ensure dignified treatment of the deceased. Maya told us the woman's English and Hebrew names. Knowing the identity ensures that the deceased is viewed as a person, not just a corpse. What I didn't know was how this woman died—a crucial factor in deciding whether or not a *taharah* is performed. For instance, purification is not always performed on a person who has died violently or a person who has many open sores and wounds.

"Are you prepared for this?" Maya asked me; I simply shrugged. We entered a small room that looked like a run-down medical office. The wrapped body was lying on a gurney. Above it was a large fan; at the feet, a large sink. The room was messy but functional. The linoleum floor and formica countertops were marbled with stains. We donned the surgical gowns and washed each hand, beginning with the right, three times from a vessel. No blessing was recited, and we let our hands dry naturally.

Maya coached me through the preparatory prayers. I stumbled over each word with the clumsiness of a young Hebrew-school student. She gently corrected my numerous mistakes. The first prayer included this woman's Hebrew name. I wondered who she was, what she did for a living, if she had children or grandchildren, what her home looked like—questions for which I would never get an answer.

We had to pay careful attention to our actions: how we washed and dried, which side of the body to wash first, which way to bring the coffin in and out of the room.

Once the washing had been completed, we began the purification of *taharah.* Three buckets of water (equal to six gallons) were filled. Our Russian teammate held the table steady as Maya and I poured a continuous stream of water from the buckets over her entire body. The instructions indicate that this must be done in tandem, and if at any point we had stopped, we would have been forced to start all over again. As we were pouring, we recited "she is pure" three times. We removed the boards that helped elevate the woman from one gurney and carefully dried her body with a clean white sheet. We then recited another prayer, which acknowledged that the deceased will be dressed in white linen shrouds, the clothes of salvation.

The body is then clothed in trousers with closed feet, a blouse, a *kittel* (robe), a face cover, and a cap. We also tied sashes below the knees and around the waist. The ties are twisted four times while reciting, "*aleph, bet, gimel, dalet,*" the names of the first four letters in the Hebrew alphabet. Each sash is tied in the form of a *shin,* a symbol for God.

Dressing the deceased woman was the most physically demanding part of *taharah.* We carefully lifted each limb as we placed the various garments on her. Her limbs felt like heavy wooden blocks. We were sweating heavily, and our breathing became deep and rapid. Except for the sound of our collective breathing, we worked in silence. When she was fully shrouded, I was moved by her beauty and her great dignity in the soft, white garments. At that moment, death began to seem benign, its mystery less inscrutable. We lined the coffin with a sheet and lifted her body with the assistance of a motor and four cloth straps. We guided the corpse into the coffin and wrapped it in the sheet.

We each took a bit of soil from Israel and scattered it over her body, dusting her closed eyes, heart, and genitals. The rest of the soil was scattered throughout the coffin. Before the lid was put on, Maya asked us to pray privately to the deceased person, to ask for forgiveness if we had done anything to hurt or offend her. For me, this was a blessed moment. It was the first and last time I was acknowledging the personal relationship between this woman and me. In my prayer, I thanked her for allowing me to perform this *mitzvah*, and then, quite spontaneously, I said silently, "I wish you well."

We placed the lid on the coffin, which, according to Jewish law, is never to be reopened under any circumstances. We said a prayer that asked for the woman's blessing and protection. Quickly and efficiently, we removed our surgical gowns and gloves and took all the equipment and supplies out of the room. As we wheeled the coffin out of the room (feet first), we recited the final prayer, which invites the angels to watch over the person in all her paths and asks that no evil come before her. We wheeled the coffin into the chapel, where it would be watched by Maya until morning.

Returning home that evening, I was struck by an intense awareness of my husband's warm body close to mine as we went to sleep. I listened to his heartbeat and the rush of blood running through his body. What surprised me even more in the following days was the way I reacted to situations that normally irritate me, like being cut off in traffic or waiting in line at the grocery store. Instead of feeling annoyed, I felt genuinely happy to be alive.

The Torah teaches care and respect for all that this world contains. Above all, it teaches that small acts of generosity can heal the greatest wounds. *Taharah* is one of those acts. As one member of the men's *taharah* said to me, "We should only treat the living so well."

An Outline of This Expanded Edition

Chapter 1 of this Expanded Edition of *Chesed Shel Emet* presents the framework for the liturgical analysis, including the methodology and discussion of several key background concepts.

Chapter 2 describes some general principles of behavior and organization that apply to the ritual.

Chapter 3 describes activities of the *m'taharim* that take place prior to beginning the ritual, first outside the *taharah* room and then inside.

Chapter 4 gives an overview of the ritual, including the five major components of the process, and outlines how Chapters 5 through 9 are organized.

Chapters 5 through 9 form the heart of the manual, and give the liturgy itself as well as descriptions of the physical actions that precede, accompany, or follow each piece of the liturgy. These chapters also include our commentary on the liturgy, as well as a set of *kavanot*—statements of intention—which we have created that might accompany each component of the liturgy to help the m'taharim understand the role of the actions and the liturgy within the liturgy.

Chapter 10 describes activities that take place after the ritual, first inside the *taharah* room and then outside.

There are also several appendices and a bibliography.

Chapter 1
How Prayer Works and Functions: Its Effect on the Person(s) Praying

In considering a specific prayer or an entire service, the reader often looks at the text(s) with a certain set of lenses. For the first time reader, the text may be viewed through the lens of translation (regardless of the language); the more advanced person may be interested in source quotations, history, use of metaphor, and the like.

Here, our focus on the text concerns three related questions:
1. What is the power that has enabled it to last all these years?
2. How does it work, in terms of its effect on the people reciting it?
3. What do the words have to do with the *met/metah* (the deceased)?

Stated differently, to what need does the liturgical piece (or service) serve as a response? The prayer thus becomes an answer to unstated or hidden questions. Our task here is to decipher the underlying needs or questions and see how the prayer responds to those needs or questions.

Ma'avar Yabok is, as far as we know, the first codification of the ritual of *taharah*. It was authored by R. Aharon Berechiah ben Moshe of Modena in 1626 in Mantua, Italy. The enormous influence of the *Kabbalah* is certainly felt, but a proper understanding of that influence waits to be written. Berechiah comments that these prayers "will increase the holiness that is needed [i.e., improve our *kavanah*] and awaken mercy."[1]

Thus, the prayers force consciousness (*kavanah*) on the one praying. They not only "awaken mercy" (from God, for us and for the *met/metah*) but also awaken *us*—from our complacency. They disturb us such that we begin to pay more attention to what we are doing. That, precisely, is one of the key purposes of this liturgy—to ward off apathy and the perfunctory recitation of the words.

---

1. From p. 1 of a translation/draft by Rabbi Dr. Steven A. Moss that has been made available as a pdf file to the Gamliel Institute.

The liturgy establishes an order through which the *m'taharim* progress. The liturgy's intense, minute descriptions tell us how to proceed, knowing that at any moment, something technical may go wrong and disrupt the smooth flow of the process. Liturgy establishes an even keel, something on which we can rely no matter whether things are going routinely or with great difficulty.

FIVE UNDERLYING CONCEPTS & SETTINGS FOR *TAHARAH*

Berechiah and many other early users of the liturgy undoubtedly had a firm grasp of a vast body of Jewish literature and lore, and it is impossible to appreciate the ritual without knowing or understanding certain parts of the background that are taken for granted in the words. Here we summarize the essential prerequisite knowledge.

1. *Tahor* and *Tamei*

The word *taharah* is used both for the overall ritual of preparation of the body for burial, as well as for the central action of this ritual, the pouring of water over the body of the *met/metah* (or the immersion of the body in a *mikveh*).

The root letters of *taharah* (*tet-hei-resh*) also form the adjective *tahor*. The concept paired with *tahor* is *tamei* (root letters *tet-mem-aleph*).

Tahor and *tamei* are often translated respectively, as "pure" and "impure" or as "clean" and "unclean." Neither of these English word pairs is adequate. In Rabbinic *halachic* literature, the term *tamei* describes something or someone that has come into contact with a primary source of *tumah* (the noun form of the word)—a corpse or anything else that reeks of death and that must be kept far removed from the presence of God in the Temple or from anything that will approach that which has been sanctified. That which is *tahor* (by having been purified, usually with flowing water) is that which can approach the holy.[2] A human corpse embodies the most extreme version of the state of being *tamei*, and the state of being *tahor* was a requirement for participation in all of the most important religious rituals in the ancient Temple.

Note: A related word is *m'taharim,* which one might explain as "the performers of the ritual of *taharah*" or "those who make the deceased *tahor.*" If we were to translate *tahor* as "pure," then the *m'taharim* are "purifiers."

---

2. Our thanks to Rabbi Richard Sarason for this formulation of the concepts.

2. *Kohen Gadol:* The High Priest of Temple Times

Unlike individuals such as Moses or the patriarchs, whom we view as chosen by God, the *Kohen Gadol* was a person who gained his position through a combination of genetic and political factors. He was a *kohen* by his birth, and was selected by the full set of *kohanim* to be the primary representative of the people of Israel and to stand in the presence of the Holy One.

Once each year, on Yom Kippur, after much preparation and fear, the *Kohen Gadol* would enter into the Holy of Holies (the most inner sanctum of the Temple courtyard), and pray for the welfare of himself, his family, and the entire Jewish people. In order to appear so intimately before the Holy One, he needed to be appropriately and specifically attired. His special clothes were one of the factors that changed the nature of this interaction between human and Divine, elevating it from a mere encounter to a unique and powerful moment.

This priestly clothing plays an important role in the *taharah* ritual. The *tachrichim* (burial garments) used to dress the *met/metah* are essentially identical with those prescribed for the *Kohen Gadol*.[3] We are thus led to construe the actions of the *m'taharim* within a larger, mythic context in which they indeed are treating the *met/metah* like the High Priest who is about to enter the presence of God.

We believe that the term *Kohen Gadol* is used as a gender-neutral metaphor in the liturgy, since this person was the only human who attained such closeness to God during life. And through the liturgy, we express our hope that the *met/metah* will also attain that closeness after death.

3. Zechariah: The Prophet Whose Words Anticipate the Return to Zion and the Renewal of the Temple Service

Zechariah lived and preached at the time when Jews living under Darius I of Persia were allowed to return to their homeland from exile in Babylonia and to restore their religious practices (roughly 520 B.C.E.). In the space of two intense years, Zechariah testifies to the dawn of a new era: God's reconciliation with Zion and the land. God forgives sins, and the priestly

---

3. Details of the High Priest's apparel on Yom Kippur are given in Leviticus 16:4. That verse is used in the *Halbashah* (Dressing) section of the liturgy (see item X— *K'tonet Bad Kodesh Yilbash,* etc.—in Chapter 8).

and lay leadership are restored, in the persons of Joshua ben Yehozadak and Zerubavel ben Shaltiel—heirs of the high priesthood and kingship respectively.[4]

In Chapter 3 of the book bearing his name, Zechariah envisions Joshua, the *Kohen Gadol*, in heaven, standing before the angel of God, with *HaSatan* ("the accuser") at his right hand. At the outset, the angel invokes God's rebuke of *HaSatan*, who apparently has just accused Joshua of being unfit for priestly service, at which point the angel calls Joshua "a brand plucked from fire."[5] The angelic attendants are then instructed to remove all the unclean garments from Joshua, and robe him in priestly vestments with a diadem on his head.

This ritual is a heavenly investiture for earthly service. The angel now testifies that if Joshua performs his priestly duties properly, he will keep his role as *Kohen Gadol* and be permitted to "move about" in the heavenly shrine.

There are two salient features in the story: the purification of Joshua, and the stipulation that his faithful service will permit him to move about the heavenly realm. The vision suggests that the *Kohen Gadol* will somehow participate in heavenly events (an idea which is also found in midrashic sources).

The text of this encounter plays a vital role in the *taharah* liturgy.[6]

4. The *Neshamah* After Death

Much has been written about the journey of the *neshamah* ("soul") after death. Essential here is the assumption, common to most of rabbinic literature, that *something* happens to the *neshamah* (which is perhaps best defined as "what makes you, you").

---

4. *The JPS Bible Commentary: Haftarot* (Philadelphia: JPS, 2002), p. 223.
5. For us today, this imagery inevitably evokes the Holocaust and its survivors.
6. See especially item IV—*Vaya'an Vayomer*—in the opening of the *Rechitzah* section of the liturgy (Chapter 6). In addition, these words from Zechariah are part of the *haftarah* for *parashat Beha'alotecha*, which contains a reference to *met mitzvah* (the obligation to bury a "found" corpse), so citing Zechariah may also conjure up that idea and its obligations in the minds of the *m'taharim*. One other interesting fact: the prophet Zechariah, whose book plays such an important role in R. Aharon Berechiah's *Ma'avar Yabok*, is identified in Zech. 1:1 as "Zechariah *ben Berechiah*." One can only speculate on this connection.

Our task as *m'taharim* is to assist the *neshamah* on this potentially dangerous journey, just as we are assisting the body on its more mundane journey. While it is fairly clear how our task is defined with regard to the body, it is less clear about the *neshamah*, and the liturgy attempts to assist us and connect the two.

5. Song of Songs

We recite verses from Song of Songs at several places during the *taharah*.[7] Over the centuries, the Song has been viewed in two ways: One perspective sees it as a poem about human love. Whether it is an anthology of love poems or a unified whole (there are scholars with each position), the Song extols the physical beauty of the human form.

In the second perspective, the Song is a symbolic tale of the love between God and the people of Israel. Rabbi Akiva himself made the claim that the Song of Songs is "holy of holies," and his support apparently resulted in the inclusion of this love poem in the Hebrew canon (Mishnah *Yadayim* 3:5). While this way of understanding the Song has largely been abandoned by modern scholars, it was likely the viewpoint of the early Kabbalists and of Berechiah. Seen through this lens, the *taharah* becomes something like a wedding, and the imagery becomes overtly poignant. The *met/metah* is about to enter an entirely new relationship—this time with God—and the glorification of the physical attributes of the *met/metah* might be seen as an attempt to help the *met/metah* find favor in God's eyes.

White (the color of the *tachrichim*) and the use of water are common symbols of the marital bond. This marriage/burial connection is amplified by the practice in some traditions of a groom wearing a *kittel* as a wedding garment and ultimately using the same garment as part of his burial shrouds.

EVOLUTION OF THE LITURGY
Rabbinic sources tell us very little about the rituals around preparation of the body for burial. Prior to *Ma'avar Yabok*, we have references only to a washing process, the use of *tachrichim*, and the efforts of Rabban Gamliel to make burial affordable[8]—but no liturgical texts.

---

7. See items V, VI, and XIIIa, in Chapters 6, 7, and 9 respectively. It also appears in Berechiah's version of item X (in Chapter 8).
8. See Babylonian Talmud, *Mo'ed Katan* 27b-28a.

5

So along comes R. Aharon Berechiah (1626), who says about his project:

> I composed new ideas and different explanations...to offer them
> as an offering and as incense in love and in reverence before the
> holy congregations, in order that it will make a way in the midst
> of the shaking worlds...a bridge from the world of change and de-
> struction with its sinful heavenly condition to be joined with the
> pleasures of Unity, Blessing, and Holiness...and will pass the fjord
> of Yabok to wrestle with the Lord, a man of war, until the dawn,
> that is resurrection for then our soul and body will no longer be
> called Jacob, but rather Israel, in that we will be a kingdom of
> priests and we will be worthy of seeing God face to face.[9]

Rabbi Steven Moss says that "these remarks and others in [Berechiah's]
introduction imply that the community as a whole, and the charitable
[*Chevra Kadisha*] groups in particular, were in need of direction which an
authoritative manual would supply. Berechiah saw his work as fulfilling this
purpose."[10]

With a few key exceptions,[11] all of the texts used in the *taharah* liturgy are
excerpts from classical Biblical and Rabbinic sources. Just as with our regular
prayer liturgy, when texts are extracted from their original position (that is,
taken *out* of the old context and placed in a *new* context), there is a presumed
intent on the part of the editor to make a specific point by selecting that
excerpt. When this is done successfully, the classical text then functions as
a powerful liturgical text, with the compiled verses often conveying ideas
distinct from what was in their original context, yet also conjuring up that
context.

Collectively, these texts—both the "composed" texts and the excerpted

9. Steven Moss, "The Attitude Toward Sickness, Dying and Death as Expressed in the
Liturgical Works *Maavor Yabok* and *Sefer Hahayiim*" (MA Thesis, Hebrew Union College-
Jewish Institute of Religion, 1974), p.4. Moss notes, in regard to the word "resurrection" in
the translation cited here, that "within the context of this work the word *m'chayei* should
actually be translated as 'immortality' rather than 'resurrection'."
10. Moss, Thesis, pp. 4-5.
11. The exceptions are (a) what we refer to below as "Preliminary Prayers" (see items I, II,
and III in Chapter 5); (b) the two-word chant *tahor hult'horah hi* ("he/she is *tahor*") in the
central piece of the ritual (see item VII in Chapter 7); and (c) the closing version of the
Mechilah prayer (item XIV in Chapter 9)

classical texts—form a symphony of words and ideas leading to an orchestrated rite. Part of our task here is to imagine what symphony Berechiah, and others later, sought to create by the choices that they made in creating our liturgy, and to understand how that symphony affects the *met/metah* and us.

There are variations in the liturgy. For our purposes, we began with the pamphlet "Regulations and Procedure including the Traditional Prayers and Translations for the Jewish Sacred Society (Chicago),"[12] which contains one example of the Ashkenazic rite.[13] Having given thought to the entire ritual, we have added and modified certain sections to create what we believe to be a more liturgically complete, as well as gender sensitive, ritual.[14]

WHAT TO LOOK FOR
In studying any Biblical or liturgical text, it is useful to consider the following (non-exhaustive) list of elements:

a. Key words. These can often be best found by simply counting the number of times a word or Hebrew root appears.

b. Context of citations. Since most of the liturgy consists of quotations taken out of context from Biblical or Rabbinic sources, one needs to consider the entire location from which the quotation was taken. Some verses have been truncated, suggesting that the earlier *m'taharim* knew the context well; thus, when the printed liturgy gave just part of a verse or chapter, the entire passage came into their mind.

c. Words with multiple meanings. Hebrew is rich in that its nouns and verbs often have meanings situated in time. For example, in Torah, the word *aron* refers to the ark carried in the desert that held the tablets of the Ten Commandments; in our time, it is the ark that holds the Torah scrolls; and in the work of the *Chevra Kadisha*, an

---

12. Published by the Jewish Sacred Society (Chicago, IL: n.d.). This publication, in turn, describes itself as done "with the aid of" several sources—see p. 28 of that booklet.
13. There are major differences in the Sephardic rite, but we will not go into the variations involved in that.
14. In several of the prayers, the text must be modified in gender where it refers to the deceased. We have included both male and female versions where needed.

aron is a casket.[15] Thus, the use of the word *aron* implicitly likens the casket to both of those other arks, and, consequently, implicitly likens the body of the deceased to the tablets or a Torah scroll.

d. Echoes. A word used in a given liturgical context can remind the reader of other places where the word appears—possibly in the Bible, in Rabbinic literature, or in other liturgy. For example, the phrase *m'chayei hametim* ("resurrection of the dead") immediately sends one back to the *Amidah,* while the entire issue of resurrection comes floating to the surface of consciousness.

We will be employing these analytical techniques as we discuss the *taharah* liturgy.

THE ENTITIES IN THE *TAHARAH* ROOM

Imagine the *Chevra Kadisha* group—the *m'taharim*—assembled in the *taharah* room. What are their needs? Who are the parties or "entities" assembled? And what does each entity need to say to, or on behalf of, another?

The ritual in the *taharah* room suggests interplay between three primary entities:

a. The *met/metah:* Of course, the body of the *met/metah* is present— we are washing it, dressing it, and placing it in the *aron.* But the liturgy tells us that the *neshamah* is also in the room with us, since we address the *met/metah*—directly when we say *Mechilah,* and indirectly, for example, while we dress the body—thus implying a consciousness in the one addressed.[16] That consciousness is the *neshamah.*

b. The *m'taharim* (the members of the *Chevra Kadisha*): Walking into the *taharah* room, and being in the presence of one who has died, is an experience of awe, wonder, and dread. We are coming into contact with the dead, a corpse, which is an *avi avot hatumah* (the "father" of all sources of ritual impurity, and the most severe form of

---

15. In modern Hebrew, an *aron* is simply a box or a closet.

16. This idea appears in Talmud as well. For example: "R' Abahu said: Everything that they say in the presence of the *met* is known [by the *met's* soul] until the top of the casket is closed." (Babylonian Talmud, *Shabbat* 152b) Other discussion of this idea appears, for instance, in *Brachot* 18a-19a.

impurity). Therefore, we need the Divine grace that is in the room. Who among those of us who have been present at a *taharah* has not wondered: When is it that I will be on the preparation table? That "terror by night" at the end of the liturgy[17] is in our minds from the very beginning.[18]

c. God: In the liturgy, we appeal to God on many levels. On behalf of the *met/metah,* we request compassion, mercy, and a safe journey. For ourselves, we ask for the strength to carry on the work we are doing, and for protection from harm that may befall us (from unnamed forces). And, implicitly, we ask for the power to keep our actions from becoming routine.

Several pieces of the liturgy can be seen very explicitly as an interaction between two of these three entities.

Beyond these three entities, we also have other "heavenly" creatures involved—both angels and demons (or, at least, demonic and dangerous forces). Both are referenced in the liturgy, and it is clear that, in the mind of the liturgist at least, they have a significant potential impact on what we do. It is beyond the scope of this paper to discuss the positive and negative forces that may underlie certain parts of the ritual, but their presence is undeniable, and reflects the great influence of the Zohar and the mystics of Tsfat.

---

17. See part XIIIa of *Hineih Mitato* in Chapter 9.
18. Rabbi Mel Glazer has suggested that whenever a *taharah* takes place, the *m'taharim* might imagine the ritual as being done not only for the *met/metah,* but also for themselves as well as for their parents.

Chapter 2
General Guidelines

PREPARING FOR A *TAHARAH*
All team members should be familiar with the procedures and prayers in this booklet. To facilitate the *taharah*, a group might enlarge and laminate the prayers and place them on a freestanding easel.

COMPOSITION OF A *TAHARAH* GROUP
The *Chevra Kadisha* is a group dedicated to serving the needs of the deceased. *Taharah* is one of these needs, and a *taharah* team is composed of members of a *Chevra Kadisha,* individually known as *m'taharim* (literally, "purifiers").

A *taharah* team generally consists of one leader (who has experience performing *taharah*) and three to four additional members. The *taharah* leader, sometimes called the *rosh* (literally, "head"), has the final say in any matters pertaining to the procedure and, when necessary, is responsible for seeking out a rabbinic consultation. No person should be present in the *taharah* room without the permission of the *rosh*.

Every *Chevra Kadisha* establishes its own criteria for membership, but tradition holds that family members do not perform *taharah* for other family members. ("Family member" is defined as the parent, child, sibling, or spouse of the deceased.) Jewish men perform *taharah* for men, and Jewish women perform *taharah* for women. If absolutely necessary, women may perform *taharah* for men. (However, men may never perform *taharah* for women.)

HEALTH PRECAUTIONS FOR *M'TAHARIM*
To safeguard the health of the *m'taharim*, avoid splashing blood and other bodily fluids into mucous membranes (eyes, nose, and mouth) or open wounds. Surgical gloves are essential. Disposable masks and goggles may also be useful. All *m'taharim* should be vaccinated against Hepatitis B.

TIME AND PLACE OF *TAHARAH*
Taharah is performed soon after a person dies and as close to the time of the funeral as possible. However, a *taharah* is never performed on Shabbat or on major Jewish holidays. If someone dies on Shabbat or a major holiday, the *Chevra Kadisha* is not officially notified until Shabbat has concluded.

DECISION-MAKING

Clearly, one cannot predict all of the situations that one might encounter while cleaning, washing, and dressing the *met/metah*. If a question arises, *m'taharim* may consult their local rabbi. However, the *rosh* generally has the authority to determine a course of action during *taharah*.

BEHAVIOR GUIDELINES FOR *M'TAHARIM*

Members of the *Chevra Kadisha* approach their task with great solemnity and respect. Here are a few basic guidelines:

- *Chevra Kadisha* members participating in a *taharah* should dress in clean, appropriate clothing.
- Team members should not converse during the *taharah* unless they are discussing the specific needs of the *met/metah.*
- At all times, it is important to respect the modesty and dignity of the *met/metah*. Therefore, *m'taharim* should keep the *met/metah* covered unless otherwise instructed.
- The *taharah* team should perform its work with care and at an unhurried pace.
- Details of the *taharah* are not to be discussed with anyone outside the team.

WHEN *TAHARAH* IS NOT PERFORMED

Taharah is usually performed on someone who has died from natural causes. If a person dies from an accident or act of violence that leaves blood spattered over his or her body and clothing, the full *taharah* procedure may be modified. Generally, the deceased remains in his or her clothing, is wrapped in a *sovev* (sheet), and is placed in an *aron*. If possible, any blood-soaked earth from the accident site should be placed in the *aron* with the *met/metah*. In some cases, only part of the *met/metah* is covered with blood, and it is possible to perform *taharah* on the remainder. Before proceeding in any such circumstance, consult a rabbi for guidance.

Chapter 3
Prior to the Ritual

There are some preliminary activities that the *m'taharim* should do prior to beginning the formal ritual, as well as activities that they do following the ritual. This chapter discusses the activities prior to the ritual, both outside the *taharah* room and inside the room. (Chapter 10 will discuss the activities that follow the ritual.)

OUTSIDE THE *TAHARAH* ROOM

It is important for team members to review their roles and acquire specific information before the *taharah* officially begins. Team members should take the following steps before entering the *taharah* room.

ᘖ Assign roles

For *taharah* to proceed smoothly, team members may wish to determine in advance:

- who will be the group leader.
- how the prayers will be read[19]: who will read them[20]; whether the prayers will be read in Hebrew, English, or both; and how, if at all, the group will incorporate the *kavanot*.
- who will hold the head of the *met/metah* during *taharah* procedures.
- who will pour the first, second, and third bucket of water used to purify the *met/metah* (see ACTION 3 of Chapter 7).

ᘖ Learn about the *met/metah*

To perform a proper *taharah*, *m'taharim* need to determine what precautions

---

19. It may be worth noting that the liturgy does not contain any formal "blessings." This may reflect the principle of *k'vod hamet*, in that the *met/metah* cannot respond to a blessing or say a blessing on his/her own. This is an example of the broader acknowledgment that *metim* cannot perform *mitzvot*, so we abstain, when possible, from performing *mitzvot* in settings (such as a cemetery) where the deceased are present and our doing *mitzvot* might be offensive to the *neshamot* of the *metim*.

20. Most of the prayers can be said either by an individual or by the group. We note two general exceptions—*Mechilah* (see Chapters 5 and 9) and *Tahor Hu/T'horah Hi* (see Chapter 7)—which are usually said by the entire group. For the rest of the liturgy, the *m'taharim* will often either designate a particular individual as the reader, or they will take turns reading different portions.

must be taken to ensure the health and safety of the *taharah* team. (This may not be clear until the body is uncovered, but some information may be available in advance.) *M'taharim* should also learn the Hebrew name of the *met/metah*. If the deceased had no Hebrew name, or if that name is unknown, use the person's English name.

✎ An optional prayer

The *m'taharim* may choose to preface their work with any of the following prayers, which might be read by individuals, read responsively, or read in unison.

> Source of kindness and compassion, whose ways are ways of mercy and truth, You have commanded us to act with loving kindness and righteousness toward the dead, and to engage in their proper burial. Grant us the courage and the strength to properly perform this work, this holy task of cleaning and washing the body, dressing the body in shrouds, and burying the deceased. Forgive us for any errors we may commit during this process. Guide our hands and hearts as we do this work, and enable us to fulfill the commandment of love. Help us see Your face in the face of the deceased, even as we see You in the faces of those who share this task with us. Source of life and death, be with us now and always.
>
> PSJC Hevra Kadisha Taharah Manual

> If a man dies, can he live again?
>   All the time of my service I wait
>   Until my replacement comes.
> You would call and I would answer You;
>   You would set Your heart on Your handiwork.
> Then You would not count my steps,
>   Or keep watch over my sin.
>
> Job 14:14-16

> But God will redeem my life from the clutches of Sheol,
>   for God will take me. *Selah*
>
> Psalms 49:16

Yet I was always with You,
　You held my right hand;
　You guided me by Your counsel
　　and let me toward honor.

PSALMS 73:23-24

❧

Whom else have I in heaven?
　And having You, I want no one on earth.
My body and mind fail;
　but God is the stay of my mind, my portion forever.

PSALMS 73:25-26

❧

Be strong and resolute, be not in fear or in dread of
them; for Adonai your God marches with you; God
will not fail you or forsake you.

DEUTERONOMY 31:6

❧

I am now going the way of all the earth. Acknowledge with all
your heart and soul that not one of the good things that Adonai
your God promised you has failed to happen; they have all come
true for you, not a single one has failed.

JOSHUA 23:14

❧

Youths may grow faint and weary,
　And young men stumble and fall;
But they who trust in Adonai shall renew their strength
　As eagles grow new plumes:
　They shall run and not grow weary,
　They shall march and not grow faint.

ISAIAH 40:30-31

❧

In old age they still produce fruit;
　they are full of sap and freshness,
attesting that Adonai is upright,
　my rock, in whom there is no wrong.

PSALMS 92:15-16

INSIDE THE *TAHARAH* ROOM

Once team members are inside the *taharah* room, they should take a few moments to ensure that all supplies, the position of the deceased, and the *aron* are in order, before beginning the ritual itself.

✎ Check supplies

Make sure that everything needed for *taharah* is present and in good condition. (See supply list in Appendix 3.) Tear up a sheet into strips or use washcloths that are provided. (Members will use these sheets or washcloths later to wash the body.)

✎ Check the *met/metah*

Make sure the deceased is properly arranged. Unless otherwise specified, the *met/metah* should be covered with a sheet at all times and placed on his or her back with the feet facing the door of the *taharah* room.

✎ Check the *aron*[21]

A Jew is generally buried in a *aron* that is wood, contains no metal, and has no lining. If any lining or straw is in the *aron*, remove it. The *aron* should also have a *Magen David* on it. If one is not present, affix it to the *aron* with wood glue at the end where the feet of the *met/metah* will be.

---

21. There is no requirement in Jewish law that an *aron* be used at all. For example, in Israel, bodies are simply dressed in *tachrichim* and placed directly in the grave. In some "green" cemeteries, the *aron* is a basket made of wicker or other natural material. The only definitive rule is that if there is an *aron*, it may not contain any metal. In this manual, we will be assuming that an *aron* is being used.

Chapter 4
The Ritual and the Liturgy: Overview

The *taharah* ritual has many parts. It is helpful to view it as consisting of five sections:

A. Preliminary prayers: This section of the liturgy establishes the framework for the relationships among the three key entities: we, the *m'taharim*; the *met/metah* (both body and soul); and God. It also sets the stage for the physical activities of body preparation. All of this part of the liturgy is "composed" (by Berechiah or others).

B. *Rechitzah* ("Washing"): These prayers accompany the "cleansing" washing of the body. From this point on, the liturgy consists almost entirely of excerpts from Biblical or Rabbinic sources. (The exceptions were listed earlier; see footnote 11.)

C. *Taharah*: These prayers frame the ritual of transition, the "purifying" washing of the body that is, by itself, called *taharah*.

D. *Halbashah* ("Dressing") and *Halanah*[22] ("Laying down"): These prayers accompany the dressing of the body and its placement in the *aron*.

E. Concluding prayers: This section includes our final address to the *met/metah*, the closing of the *aron,* and several concluding verses.

The word *taharah* is used both to refer to the entire ritual as well as the third of the five sections of that ritual—*taharah*, or purification—as listed above, and sometimes is used even more narrowly to mean the "pouring of water" that is central to that section (see Chapter 7).

Chapters 5–9 present the components of the *taharah* ritual itself—both the physical actions taken by the *m'taharim* with the *met/metah* and the accompanying liturgy. These five chapters correspond to the five major sections of the ritual listed above.

---

22. Placement of the body in the *aron* is also known as "*Hashkavah*." The term *Halanah* is sometimes used to refer to a traditional practice of moving the *met/metah* from the bed to the ground.

These five chapters each have several components:

- **CHAPTER OVERVIEW**
- **ACTIONS**—Descriptions, with detail as needed, of the physical actions of the ritual. These actions are numbered sequentially, starting with 1 within each chapter. Some of these actions have multiple components.
- **PRAYERS**—Texts of each of the prayers, including Hebrew, transliteration, and translation, with separate male and female versions for those prayers that require them. These elements are labeled with Roman numbers, I through XV, in one sequence for the entire ritual. Each prayer is named by the opening word or words of the text, and has an accompanying phrase describing its function in the ritual.
- *KAVANOT*—Brief statements that might be recited by the leader (or another of the *m'taharim*) preceding each prayer, explaining the essence of *that* prayer for the *m'taharim*.
- **COMMENTARY**—An explanation of the liturgical meaning and usage of each prayer and the role it plays in regard to the "entities" in the room.
- **CHAPTER SUMMARY**

Chapter 5
The Ritual and the Liturgy: Preliminary Prayers

CHAPTER OVERVIEW

This section of the liturgy establishes the framework for the relationship among the primary entities in the *taharah* room. It also sets the stage for the physical activities of preparation of the body.

ACTION 1

Once inside the *taharah* room, wash hands and put on special clothing.

ꙍ **Wash hands:** *M'taharim* wash each of their hands three times, alternating between the right and left hand and beginning with the right one. Use a hand-washing cup or other vessel to pour the water, do not recite a *brachah,* and allow hands to air dry completely (so that gloves will go on easily).

ꙍ **Put on special clothing:** After washing their hands, *m'taharim* should put on gowns, gloves, masks, goggles, and shoe covers. Some *Chevra Kadisha* groups use other protective gear.

ACTION 2

Gather around the *met/metah* and recite *Mechilah* as a group, asking forgiveness from the *met/metah*.

> **I. *MECHILAH*:**[23] **We begin the ritual of *taharah* by addressing the *met/metah*.**

> > *Kavanah*: _____ [name of the deceased], we stand here ready to begin our work. Before we do so, we ask your

23. There is a tradition of asking for *mechilah* (forgiveness) from the *met/metah* at the end of *taharah*. However, since liturgical texts often provide a frame in which what is said at the beginning is restated (perhaps in a different form) at the end, we believe that it makes sense to include both an opening *Mechilah* prayer (stated in the future tense: "forgive us for what we *may do* wrong") and a closing *Mechilah* (stated in the past tense: "forgive us for what we *may have done* wrong"). Both the opening and closing *Mechilah* are given only in English because there does not seem to be a traditional Hebrew text.

19

understanding that we will do our best to
prepare you for your final journey.

_____, ben/bat [son/daughter of]
_____ v' [and] _____, we ask
your forgiveness for any distress we may cause you
during this *taharah*. We will do everything possible
to ensure that you are treated with respect, and that
all the elements of *taharah* are properly completed.
Everything we are about to do is for the sake of your
honor.[24]

COMMENTARY

In *Mechilah*, we, the *taharah* team members, ask forgiveness
from the *met/metah*, in case we might accidentally do
anything inappropriate while performing the ritual. Although
we recite the prayer as a group, the request comes from each
of us individually. This prayer (along with *Ana Elohei* later)
serves as an "advance protection" for the *m'taharim* against
any harm that may come to us as a result of what we do, and
helps to allay our fear sufficiently so that we will have the
audacity to proceed.

It is essential to note that the *m'taharim* address the *met/metah*
directly, implying that the deceased's *neshamah* is present
and aware of what is happening, a well-established belief in
Rabbinic theology[25]. We are not simply performing a ritual
on a body, but we are concerned with the transition that
the *neshamah* is making. There is even a practice in Israel of
directly addressing the *neshamah* in the second person when
delivering a eulogy.

ACTION 3

Recite *Chamol,* pleading with God to have mercy on the *neshamah* of the *met/
metah*.

---

24. From *PSJC Hevra Kadisha Taharah Manual*, 2nd ed. (Brooklyn, NY: Park Slope Jewish
Center, 2009).
25. See references in footnote 16.

II. *CHAMOL:* We recite our first prayer to God, speaking to God on behalf of the deceased.

> *Kavanah:*[26] God, we are acting on behalf of the *neshamah* of _____ [name of the deceased], asking You for compassion and mercy on his/her behalf.

For a male:[27]

Ribono shel olam chamol al	רִבּוֹנוֹ שֶׁל עוֹלָם חֲמוֹל עַל
_____ ben _____	בֶּן _____
hamet halaz shehu ben Avraham,	הַמֵּת הַלָּז שֶׁהוּא בֶּן אַבְרָהָם,
Yitzchak, Ya'akov, Sarah, Rivkah,	יִצְחָק, יַעֲקֹב, שָׂרָה, רִבְקָה,
Rachel, v'Leah avadecha, v'tanu'ach	רָחֵל, וְלֵאָה עֲבָדֶיךָ, וְתָנוּחַ
nafsho v'nishmato im hatzadikim ki	נַפְשׁוֹ וְנִשְׁמָתוֹ עִם הַצַּדִּיקִים כִּי
Atah m'chayeh hametim umeimit	אַתָּה מְחַיֶּה הַמֵּתִים וּמֵמִית
chayim. Baruch Atah mochel v'solei'ach	חַיִּים. בָּרוּךְ אַתָּה מוֹחֵל וְסוֹלֵחַ
lachata'im v'la'avonot mimeitei amcha	לַחֲטָאִים וְלַעֲוֹנוֹת מִמֵּתֵי עַמְּךָ
Yisra'el b'tachanunim.	יִשְׂרָאֵל בְּתַחֲנוּנִים.

---

26. An alternative *kavanah*, suggested by Rabbi Edward Feld, is as follows: "We return the soul of the deceased to You. May You have compassion on it. We return the body which carried that soul to the earth from which it came. As we purify the body for burial, so may the soul of [name of the deceased] be considered pure in Your eyes."

27. In editions of *Ma'avar Yabok* available to us, most of the occurrences of the word בְּרַחֲמִים or its variants (e.g לְרַחֲמֶיךָ), in *Chamol* appear with very small Hebrew letters (א, ב, etc.) next to them as if Berechiah were counting the appearances of this word root. At the end of the third paragraph (i.e., the paragraph just for men), there is an ambiguous indication that may mean that the word בְּרַחֲמִים is to be said twice, but perhaps Berechiah is simply noting that this word will appear again as the first word of the next sentence. Some modern *taharah* manuals [e.g., JSS (see footnote 12); Schlingenbaum (see footnote 32); and Epstein (see footnote 36)] do actually repeat the word at the end of the paragraph just for men. It may also be that there is mystical significance to the number of times the word root is used.

Uv'chen y'hi ratzon milfanecha Adonai
Eloheinu veilohei avoteinu v'imoteinu
shet'sabev mal'achei rachamim lifnei
hamet, shehu avd'cha ben amatecha.
V'Atah Adonai Eloheinu v'Elohei
avoteinu v'imoteinu maskil el dal
malteihu mikol tzarah umiyom ra'ah
umidinah shel gehinom. Baruch Atah
g'dol hachesed uva'al harachamim.
Baruch Atah ha'oseh shalom bimromav
la'avadav ul'yirei sh'mo. Baruch
podeh amo Yisra'el miminei pur'aniyot
b'rachamim.

וּבְכֵן יְהִי רָצוֹן מִלְּפָנֶיךָ יְיָ
אֱלֹהֵינוּ וֵאלֹהֵי אֲבוֹתֵנוּ וְאִמּוֹתֵינוּ
שֶׁתְּסַבֵּב מַלְאֲכֵי רַחֲמִים לִפְנֵי
הַמֵּת, שֶׁהוּא עַבְדְּךָ בֶּן אֲמָתֶךָ.
וְאַתָּה יְיָ אֱלֹהֵינוּ וֵאלֹהֵי
אֲבוֹתֵנוּ וְאִמּוֹתֵינוּ מַשְׂכִּיל אֶל דָּל
מַלְּטֵהוּ מִכָּל צָרָה וּמִיּוֹם רָעָה
וּמִדִּינָה שֶׁל גֵּיהִנֹּם. בָּרוּךְ אַתָּה
גְּדוֹל הַחֶסֶד וּבַעַל הָרַחֲמִים.
בָּרוּךְ אַתָּה הָעֹשֶׂה שָׁלוֹם בִּמְרוֹמָיו
לַעֲבָדָיו וְלִירְאֵי שְׁמוֹ. בָּרוּךְ
פּוֹדֶה עַמּוֹ יִשְׂרָאֵל מִמִּינֵי פֻּרְעָנִיּוֹת
בְּרַחֲמִים.

Uv'chen y'hi ratzon milfanecha Adonai
Eloheinu v'Elohei avoteinu v'imoteinu
shetizkor z'chut b'rit kodesh shebivsaro
v'yihyeh pidyon lo mis'refat gehinom
v'tachalitzeihu. Baruch Atah koret
habrit b'rachamim.

וּבְכֵן יְהִי רָצוֹן מִלְּפָנֶיךָ יְיָ
אֱלֹהֵינוּ וֵאלֹהֵי אֲבוֹתֵנוּ וְאִמּוֹתֵינוּ
שֶׁתִּזְכּוֹר זְכוּת בְּרִית קֹדֶשׁ שֶׁבִּבְשָׂרוֹ
וְיִהְיֶה פִּדְיוֹן לוֹ מִשְׂרֵפַת גֵּיהִנֹּם
וְתַחַלִּיצֵהוּ. בָּרוּךְ אַתָּה כּוֹרֵת
הַבְּרִית בְּרַחֲמִים.

B'rachamim haster v'ha'aleim pish'ei
hamet hazeh avdecha. Misreifat
eish tachalitzeihu shehu tzarich
l'rachamecha harabim. V'Atah Adonai
Eloheinu tov v'salach l'chol kor'echa.
Baruch Atah g'dol ha'eitzah v'rav

בְּרַחֲמִים הַסְתֵּר וְהַעֲלֵם פִּשְׁעֵי
הַמֵּת הַזֶּה עַבְדֶּךָ. מִשְׂרֵפַת
אֵשׁ תַּחַלִּיצֵהוּ שֶׁהוּא צָרִיךְ
לְרַחֲמֶיךָ הָרַבִּים. וְאַתָּה יְיָ
אֱלֹהֵינוּ טוֹב וְסַלָּח לְכָל קוֹרְאֶיךָ.
בָּרוּךְ אַתָּה גְּדוֹל הָעֵצָה וְרַב

ha'aliliyah b'rachamim. Im raglei	הָעֲלִילִיָה בְּרַחֲמִים. עִם רַגְלֵי
tzadikim b'gan eden yidroch, ki m'kom	צַדִּיקִים בְּגַן עֵדֶן יִדְרוֹךְ, כִּי מְקוֹם
y'sharim hu raglei chasidav yishmor.	יְשָׁרִים הוּא רַגְלֵי חֲסִידָיו יִשְׁמוֹר.
Baruch Atah hanotein rachamim	בָּרוּךְ אַתָּה הַנּוֹתֵן רַחֲמִים
g'dolim v'rov tachanunim l'meitei amo	גְדוֹלִים וְרוֹב תַּחֲנוּנִים לְמֵתֵי עַמּוֹ
Yisra'el. Amen, ken y'hi ratzon.	יִשְׂרָאֵל. אָמֵן, כֵּן יְהִי רָצוֹן.

Ruler of the universe! Have compassion for
_____, the son of _____ and
_____, this deceased, for he is a descendant
of Abraham, Isaac, Jacob, Sarah, Rebecca, Rachel,
and Leah, Your servants. May his soul and spirit rest
with the righteous, for You revive the dead and bring
death to the living. Blessed are You who pardons and
forgives the sins and trespasses of the dead of Your
people, on petition.

Therefore, may it be Your will, Adonai our God and
God of our ancestors, to encircle angels of mercy
around the deceased, for he is Your servant and son
of Your maidservant. And You, Adonai our God and
God of our ancestors, who is concerned with the
poor, save him from all misery, from a day of evil, and
from judgment to *Gehenna*. Blessed are You, great
in lovingkindness and provider of mercy. Blessed are
You who makes peace in the heights for Your servants
and for those who revere Your name. Blessed is the
One who redeems the people Israel from all suffering
through mercy.

Therefore, may it be Your will, Adonai our God and
God of our ancestors, to remember the merit of the
sacred covenant which is in his flesh, and may it be for
him a ransom from the fires of *Gehenna*, so that You
may deliver him. Blessed are You who establishes the
covenant through mercy.

Through mercy, hide and ignore the transgressions of this deceased, Your servant. Deliver him from consumption by fire, for he needs Your great mercy. And You, Adonai our God, are good and forgiving to all who call upon You. Blessed are You, mercifully great in counsel and mighty in achievement. May he tread with the feet of the righteous in the Garden of Eden, for that is the place of the upright. God protects the feet of the pious. Blessed are You who gives great mercy and abundant grace to the deceased of Your people Israel. Amen. May such be God's will.

For a female:

Ribono shel olam chamol al	רִבּוֹנוֹ שֶׁל עוֹלָם חֲמוֹל עַל
_____ *bat* _____	בַּת _____ _____
hametah halazo shehi bat Avraham,	הַמֵּתָה הַלָּזוֹ שֶׁהִיא בַּת אַבְרָהָם,
Yitzhak, Ya'akov, Sarah, Rivkah,	יִצְחָק, יַעֲקֹב, שָׂרָה, רִבְקָה,
Rachel, v'Leah avadecha, v'tanu'ach	רָחֵל, וְלֵאָה עֲבָדֶיךָ, וְתָנוּחַ
nafshah v'nishmatah im hatzadikim	נַפְשָׁה וְנִשְׁמָתָה עִם הַצַּדִּיקִים
ki Atah m'chayeh hametim umeimit	כִּי אַתָּה מְחַיֶּה הַמֵּתִים וּמֵמִית
chayim. Baruch Atah mochel v'solei'ach	חַיִּים. בָּרוּךְ אַתָּה מוֹחֵל וְסוֹלֵחַ
lachata'im v'la'avonot mimeitei amcha	לַחֲטָאִים וְלַעֲוֹנוֹת מִמֵּתֵי עַמְּךָ
Yisra'el b'tachanunim.	יִשְׂרָאֵל בְּתַחֲנוּנִים.
Uv'chen y'hi ratzon milfanecha Adonai	וּבְכֵן יְהִי רָצוֹן מִלְּפָנֶיךָ יְיָ
Eloheinu v'Elohei avoteinu v'imoteinu	אֱלֹהֵנוּ וֵאלֹהֵי אֲבוֹתֵנוּ וְאִמּוֹתֵינוּ
shet'sabev mal'achei rachamim lifnei	שֶׁתְּסַבֵּב מַלְאֲכֵי רַחֲמִים לִפְנֵי
hametah, shehi amatcha bat amatecha.	הַמֵּתָה, שֶׁהִיא עֲמָתְךָ בַּת אֲמָתֶךָ.
V'Atah Adonai Eloheinu v'Elohei	וְאַתָּה יְיָ אֱלֹהֵנוּ וֵאלֹהֵי
avoteinu v'imoteinu maskil el dal	אֲבוֹתֵנוּ וְאִמּוֹתֵינוּ מַשְׂכִּיל אֶל דָּל

24

malteha mikol tzarah umiyom ra'ah
umidinah shel gehinom. Baruch Atah
g'dol hachesed uva'al harachamim.
Baruch Atah ha'oseh shalom bimromav
la'avadav ul'yirei sh'mo. Baruch
podeh amo Yisra'el miminei pur'aniyot
b'rachamim.

B'rachamim haster v'ha'aleim pish'ei
hametah hazot amatecha. Misreifat
eish tachalitzeiha shehi tzrichah
l'rachamecha harabim. V'Atah Adonai
Eloheinu tov v'salach l'chol kor'echa.
Baruch Atah g'dol ha'eitzah v'rav
ha'aliliyah b'rachamim. Im raglei
tzadikim b'gan eden tidroch, ki m'kom
y'sharim hu raglei chasidav yishmor.
Baruch Atah hanotein rachamim
g'dolim v'rov tachanunim l'meitei amo
Yisra'el. Amen, ken y'hi ratzon.

מַלְּטָהּ מִכָּל צָרָה וּמִיּוֹם רָעָה
וּמִדִּינָהּ שֶׁל גֵּיהִנֹּם. בָּרוּךְ אַתָּה
גְּדוֹל הַחֶסֶד וּבַעַל הָרַחֲמִים.
בָּרוּךְ אַתָּה הָעֹשֶׂה שָׁלוֹם בִּמְרוֹמָיו
לַעֲבָדָיו וּלְיִרְאֵי שְׁמוֹ. בָּרוּךְ
פּוֹדֶה עַמּוֹ יִשְׂרָאֵל מִמִּינֵי פּוּרְעָנִיּוֹת
בְּרַחֲמִים.

בְּרַחֲמִים הַסְתֵּר וְהַעֲלֵם פִּשְׁעֵי
הַמֵּתָה הַזֹּאת אֲמָתֶךָ. מִשְׂרֵפַת
אֵשׁ תַּחַלִּיצֶהָ שֶׁהִיא צְרִיכָה
לְרַחֲמֶיךָ הָרַבִּים. וְאַתָּה יְיָ
אֱלֹהֵינוּ טוֹב וְסַלָּח לְכָל קוֹרְאֶיךָ.
בָּרוּךְ אַתָּה גְּדוֹל הָעֵצָה וְרַב
הָעֲלִילִיָּה בְּרַחֲמִים. עִם רַגְלֵי
צַדִּיקִים בְּגַן עֵדֶן תִּדְרוֹךְ, כִּי מְקוֹם
יְשָׁרִים הוּא רַגְלֵי חֲסִידָיו יִשְׁמוֹר.
בָּרוּךְ אַתָּה הַנּוֹתֵן רַחֲמִים
גְּדוֹלִים וְרוֹב תַּחֲנוּנִים לְמֵתֵי עַמּוֹ
יִשְׂרָאֵל. אָמֵן, כֵּן יְהִי רָצוֹן.

Ruler of the universe! Have compassion for
_____, the daughter of _____ and
_____, this deceased, for she is a descendant
of Abraham, Isaac, Jacob, Sarah, Rebecca, Rachel,
and Leah, Your servants. May her soul and spirit rest
with the righteous, for You revive the dead and bring
death to the living. Blessed are You who pardons and
forgives, on petition, the sins and trespasses of the
dead of Your people.

Therefore, may it be Your will, Adonai our God and God of our ancestors, to encircle angels of mercy around the deceased, for she is Your servant and daughter of Your maidservant. And You, Adonai our God and God of our ancestors, who is concerned with the poor, save her from all misery, from a day of evil, and from judgment to *Gehenna*. Blessed are You, great in lovingkindness and provider of mercy. Blessed are You who makes peace in the heights for Your servants and for those who revere Your name. Blessed is the One who mercifully redeems the people Israel from all suffering.

Through mercy, hide and ignore the transgressions of this deceased, Your servant. Deliver her from consumption by fire, for she needs Your great mercy. And You, Adonai our God, are good and forgiving to all who call upon You. Blessed are You, mercifully great in counsel and mighty in achievement. May she tread with the feet of the righteous in the Garden of Eden, for that is the place of the upright. God protects the feet of the pious. Blessed are You who gives great mercy and abundant grace to the deceased of Your people Israel. Amen. May such be God's will.

COMMENTARY

After speaking directly to the deceased, the *m'taharim* now turn to address God. We speak to God on behalf of the deceased, asking for compassion, invoking *z'chut avot* (the merit of the ancestors) and, for men, the sign of the *brit*.[28] For a male, the implication is: since the deceased entered into this covenant with You (God), You have an obligation to have mercy on him.

We don't know what will happen next to the *neshamah* (for example, we read that the deceased needs protection from "all misery" and from "judgment to *Gehenna*"). This is frightening

---

28. Some *Chevra Kadisha* groups have a tradition of performing a *brit* when they do a *taharah* for a male who is uncircumcised.

even to us, and so we ask God for the best of outcomes for the *met/metah*.

In seeking God's mercy for the *met/metah*, we praise God's nature (e.g., "great in lovingkindness" and "provider of mercy"), as we are calling upon God to feel obligated to provide this mercy. We even seek protection for the deceased through "angels of mercy" (perhaps to argue the case of the *met/metah* before God?). We have here the verb *t'sovev*— "encircle"—as if God were "wrapping" the angels around the *met/metah*. The root of this verb occurs later as the *sovev*, or "winding sheet," that encircles the *met/metah* in the *aron*, and also in part XIIIa of *Hineih Mitato* (in Chapter 9).

In a bit of circularity, this prayer (which Berechiah presumably composed) requires by its own language that it be said. It asserts that God forgives "on petition" (*b'tachanunim*). If God must be petitioned in order that forgiveness be granted, then it becomes our obligation to make that petition on behalf of the *met/metah*—hence, we recite *Chamol*.

Looking further at the language of *Chamol*, the topic of the prayer becomes clear simply from the repetition of certain words within it. We have the following word counts:

- *Atah* ("You"): directly addressing God – 9 occurrences
- *rachem*, or words with the same root ("mercy"): a plea to God to have compassion – 8 occurrences (or maybe 9; see footnote 27)
- *met/metah* ("deceased") – 7 occurrences
- *Baruch* ("blessed"): directly referencing God – 7 occurrences
- *Gehinom* (*Gehenna*, "the netherworld"): the greatest "danger" for the *met/metah* – 2 occurrences

Note: While *Baruch Atah* is a phrase used six times, it is an incomplete *brachah* formula.[29]

---

29. A complete *brachah* includes the formula "*Baruch Atah, Adonai Eloheinu, Melech ha'olam*" at its beginning.

We have set the prayer in paragraphs, as suggested by the word *uv'chen*, which appears twice in the male form of the prayer and once in the female form. This word suggests a new thought, and creates a symphonic thematic crescendo. The prayer ends with a glorious conclusion: *amen, ken y'hi ratzon.*

Throughout, we hear echoes from other liturgical contexts, stretching our thoughts back to other instances in our liturgy [such as, for example, *m'chayeh hametim* ("revive the dead"), from the *Amidah*; *maskil el dal* ("concerned with the poor"), from Psalm 91; *tov v'salach l'chol kor'echa* ("good and forgiving to all who call upon You"), from High Holiday liturgy; and *g'dol ha'eitzah v'rav ha'aliliyah* ("great in counsel and mighty in achievement"), from *Tzidduk haDin* (in the funeral service)] as well as to important themes (such as, for example, *Gehinom* – the netherworld; and *Gan Eden* – the Garden of Eden).

The title of the prayer, *Chamol,* gives us the general theme. Yet the word itself appears only once. By inverting its root letters, *chet-mem-lamed*, one moves from "have compassion" to *mem-chet-lamed*, "forgive"—a possible subtle linguistic ploy that brings us back to our opening *Mechilah* prayer.

Finally, it must be acknowledged that there is a personal undercurrent in saying *Chamol.* Whenever we perform the *taharah* ritual, we are acknowledging (either consciously or not) that, at some point in time, we too will be lying on the table and another group of *m'taharim* will be intoning these same words. Thus, we are at once asking for mercy on behalf of the *neshamah* and also becoming aware ourselves of the fragility of life.

ACTION 4
Recite *Ana Elohei,* asking God for the courage and strength to perform *taharah* properly.

III. *ANA ELOHEI:*[30] We ask God to give us strength and keep us from harm.

Kavanah: God, give us the strength to do our work properly, keep us from harm, and give us heightened awareness of what we are doing.

For a male:

Ana Elohei hachesed v'harachamim,
shekol orchotecha chesed v'emet,
v'tzivitanu la'asot chesed v'emet im
hametim ul'hit'asek bikvuratam,
k'mo shekatuv: "Ki kavur
tikb'renu."

אָנָּא אֱלֹהֵי הַחֶסֶד וְהָרַחֲמִים,
שֶׁכָּל אוֹרְחוֹתֶיךָ חֶסֶד וֶאֱמֶת,
וְצִוִּיתָנוּ לַעֲשׂוֹת חֶסֶד וֶאֱמֶת עִם
הַמֵּתִים וּלְהִתְעַסֵּק בִּקְבוּרָתָם,
כְּמוֹ שֶׁכָּתוּב: "כִּי קָבוֹר
תִּקְבְּרֶנוּ" (דברים כא:כג).

Uv'chen y'hi ratzon milfanecha, Adonai
Eloheinu, shet'am'tzeinu ut'chaz'keinu
la'asot m'lachteinu m'lechet shamayim
zo k'ra'ui, hen b'tohorat hamet, hen
bilvishato uvikvurato, v'tishm'renu
mikol nezek ut'kalah, shelo nikasheil
b'ma'aseh yadeinu.

וּבְכֵן יְהִי רָצוֹן מִלְּפָנֶיךָ, יהוה
אֱלֹהֵינוּ, שֶׁתְּאַמְּצֵנוּ וּתְחַזְּקֵנוּ
לַעֲשׂוֹת מְלַאכְתֵּנוּ מְלֶאכֶת שָׁמַיִם
זוֹ כָּרָאוּי, הֵן בְּטָהֳרַת הַמֵּת, הֵן
בִּלְבִישָׁתוֹ וּבִקְבוּרָתוֹ, וְתִשְׁמְרֵנוּ
מִכָּל נֶזֶק וּתְקָלָה, שֶׁלֹּא נִכָּשֵׁל
בְּמַעֲשֵׂה יָדֵינוּ.

L'kayem banu hamikra "Shomer
mitzvah lo yeida davar ra."
V'ta'amod lanu z'chut mitzvat g'milut
chesed v'emet l'mal'ot yamenu b'tovah.
V'chesed Adonai aleinu l'olam.

לְקַיֵּם בָּנוּ הַמִּקְרָא "שׁוֹמֵר
מִצְוָה לֹא יֵדַע דָּבָר רָע" (קהלת ח:ה).
וְתַעֲמֹד לָנוּ זְכוּת מִצְוַת גְּמִילוּת
חֶסֶד וֶאֱמֶת לְמַלֹּאת יָמֵינוּ בְּטוֹבָה.
וְחֶסֶד יהוה עָלֵינוּ לְעוֹלָם.

---

30. *Ana Elohei* does not appear in *Ma'avar Yabok*, nor in many of our contemporary *taharah* manuals, but it was used in J.D. Eisenstein, *Mourner's Manual: Customs and Services in the House of Mourning* (NY: Hebrew Publishing Company, 1929).

29

O God of lovingkindness and compassion, all of whose ways are lovingkindness and truth, You have commanded us to practice lovingkindness and truth with the dead, and to attend to their burial, as it is written, "you shall surely bury him" (DEUTERONOMY 21:23).

Therefore, Adonai our God, may it be Your will to give us courage and strength to do our task, this heavenly task, as appropriate, whether in performing *taharah* for the *met*, or in dressing him, or burying him. And keep us from any injury or obstacle such that the work of our hands not be disrupted.

Sustain in us the statement: "One who observes a *mitzvah* encounters no evil" (ECCLESIASTES 8:5). Establish for us the privilege of the *mitzvah* of *gemilut chesed v'emet*, that it fills our days with goodness. And may God's lovingkindness be upon us forever.

For a female:

Ana Elohei hachesed v'harachamim,
shekol orchotecha chesed v'emet,
v'tzivitanu la'asot chesed v'emet im
hametim ul'hit'asek bikvuratam,
k'mo shekatuv: "Ki kavur
tikb'renu."

אָנָּא אֱלֹהֵי הַחֶסֶד וְהָרַחֲמִים,
שֶׁכָּל אוֹרְחוֹתֶיךָ חֶסֶד וֶאֱמֶת,
וְצִוִּיתָנוּ לַעֲשׂוֹת חֶסֶד וֶאֱמֶת עִם
הַמֵּתִים וּלְהִתְעַסֵּק בִּקְבוּרָתָם,
כְּמוֹ שֶׁכָּתוּב: "כִּי קָבוֹר
תִּקְבְּרֶנוּ" (דברים כא:כג).

Uv'chen y'hi ratzon milfanecha, Adonai
Eloheinu, shet'am'tzeinu ut'chaz'keinu
la'asot m'lachteinu m'lechet shamayim
zo k'ra'ui, hen b'tohorat hametah, hen
bilvishatah uvikvuratah, v'tishm'renu

וּבְכֵן יְהִי רָצוֹן מִלְּפָנֶיךָ, יהוה
אֱלֹהֵינוּ, שֶׁתְּאַמְּצֵנוּ וּתְחַזְּקֵנוּ
לַעֲשׂוֹת מְלַאכְתֵּנוּ מְלֶאכֶת שָׁמַיִם
זוֹ כָּרָאוּי, הֵן בְּטָהֳרַת הַמֵּתָה, הֵן
בִּלְבִישָׁתָה וּבִקְבוּרָתָה, וְתִשְׁמְרֵנוּ

mikol nezek ut'kalah shelo nikasheil
b'ma'aseh yadeinu.

מִכָּל נֶזֶק וּתְקָלָה, שֶׁלֹא נִכָּשֵׁל
בְּמַעֲשֵׂה יָדֵינוּ.

L'kayem banu hamikra "Shomer
mitzvah lo yeida davar ra."
V'ta'amod lanu z'chut mitzvat g'milut
chesed v'emet l'mal'ot yamenu b'tovah.
V'chesed Adonai aleinu l'olam.

לְקַיֵּם בָּנוּ הַמִּקְרָא ״שׁוֹמֵר
מִצְוָה לֹא יֵדַע דָּבָר רָע״ (קהלת ח:ה).
וְתַעֲמֹד לָנוּ זְכוּת מִצְוַת גְּמִילוּת
חֶסֶד וֶאֱמֶת לְמַלֹּאת יָמֵינוּ בְּטוֹבָה.
וְחֶסֶד יהוה עָלֵינוּ לְעוֹלָם.

O God of lovingkindness and compassion, all of
whose ways are lovingkindness and truth, You have
commanded us to practice lovingkindness and truth
with the dead, and to attend to their burial, as it is
written, "you shall surely bury him" (DEUTERONOMY
21:23).

Therefore, Adonai our God, may it be Your will to
give us courage and strength to do our task, this
heavenly task, as appropriate, whether in performing
taharah for the *metah*, or in dressing her, or burying
her. And keep us from any injury or obstacle such that
the work of our hands not be disrupted.

Sustain in us the statement: "One who observes a
mitzvah encounters no evil" (ECCLESIASTES 8:5). Establish
for us the privilege of the *mitzvah* of *gemilut chesed
v'emet,* that it fills our days with goodness. And may
God's lovingkindness be upon us forever.

COMMENTARY

This prayer opens by citing Torah to establish that our work
is in (partial) fulfillment of God's commandment: "you
shall surely bury him." In citing this verse, we remind both
ourselves and God that we are performing a *mitzvah*. We
thus deserve the protection that this status provides: "one

31

who observes a *mitzvah* encounters no evil."[31] This right to protection is also alluded to in the phrase *v'ta'amod lanu z'chut mitzva[h]* ("Establish for us the privilege of the *mitzvah*").

By carrying out the *taharah* portion of the burial process, we are also acting in imitation of God, as it says in the Babylonian Talmud (*Sotah* 14a), "The Holy One, Blessed is the One, buried the dead, as it is written, 'He [God] buried him [Moses] in the valley' (DEUTERONOMY 34:6). You too should bury the dead."

But identifying our work as a *mitzvah* also emphasizes that we must do our work with full *kavanah*, and *Ana Elohei* is therefore, at least implicitly, a plea that our work not become mechanical. We must perform the task as appropriate— *k'ra'ui*—and so that our work not fail—*shelo nikasheil*. For those who perform this *mitzvah* frequently, routinization may be our greatest fear and the greatest danger. *Ana Elohei* helps prevent this from happening.

Some other connections:
- The words *v'harachamim* and *uv'chen* connect us to the earlier *Chamol,* while the words *taharah* and *bilvishato* ("in dressing him") project us forward to what we are about to do.
- The phrase *chesed v'emet* ("lovingkindness and truth") appears three times. (In the third appearance, toward the end, we left it untranslated.) It refers to the way in which we should be observing the *mitzvah*—with steadfast loyalty. The phrase is used in *Ana Elohei* to describe both our work and God's.

CHAPTER SUMMARY
We are now ready to move from the "getting acquainted" stage of the liturgy to the action stage. In particular, this means confronting the reality of the

---

31. See, for instance, Babylonian Talmud, *Sotah* 21a. A familiar instance of this idea is the practice of giving money to a traveler to Israel, asking the traveler to act as a messenger to use the money to provide *tzedakah* for the needy there. The traveler's journey is thus part of the performance of a *mitzvah,* which affords protection to the traveler.

dead body. Perhaps these preliminary prayers, and especially *Ana Elohei,* are designed to temper the upcoming shock of that encounter, especially for a person doing his or her first *taharah*; and these preliminary prayers may also prevent routinization for the person doing *taharah* for the 100th time.

Chapter 6
The Ritual and the Liturgy: *Rechitzah*

CHAPTER OVERVIEW
Rechitzah is the second step in the *taharah* ritual. It is composed of three main parts:

- Reciting *Vaya'an Vayomer,* which sets the stage for the physical cleaning or washing of the *met/metah* by invoking Zechariah's vision. (The "ritual" washing takes place in Chapter 7.)
- The physical washing itself.
- Reciting *Rosho Ketem Paz* (for a male) or *Hinach Yafah* (for a female), which praise the physical body of the *met/metah*.

We provide here general guidelines about washing the *met/metah,* which the group should understand before beginning.

ᘐ General guidelines for washing the *met/metah*
M'taharim should be familiar with certain guidelines before they begin to wash the *met/metah*. First, it is important to protect the dignity and modesty of the *met/metah* by keeping his or her genitals covered at all times. During *Rechitzah,* the genitals are uncovered only so that the *m'taharim* can wash them. Second, members should be careful to not bend or close any fingers or other joints of the *met/metah* while washing them. Third, blood and bodily discharges must be handled very carefully when the *met/metah* is being washed, and dressings and tubes also require special care. Here are specific instructions:

> **Blood:** Do not wash away blood that flowed at the time of death. *M'taharim* may wash away any blood that flowed while the person was alive, including blood from wounds or blood resulting from an operation. In practice, it can be very difficult to differentiate between blood that flowed at the time of death and blood that flowed before death occurred. Therefore, it is customary to wash off all blood that is on the deceased. Any cloths used for this purpose should be placed in the *aron* and buried with the *met/metah*. Monsel's solution (ferric sub-sulfate solution) is recommended by some to help stop bleeding. If blood continues to flow

from a wound or opening, and it is not possible to stop the flow within a reasonable period of time, apply a fresh bandage to the wound to prevent further discharge.

Bowel discharges: Wash off any discharges that do not contain visible amounts of blood. If discharges or seepages persist, place a diaper on the *met/metah* to contain the flow.

Dressings and tubes: *M'taharim* may leave intact dressings on the *met/metah*. Remove tubes and bags (but only if sufficiently knowledgeable to be able to do so without damaging the *met/metah*—otherwise, leave them intact). Collect any bloodied bandages or diapers that have been removed from the *met/metah* and place them in the *aron*. Be careful not to tear the skin while removing bandages.

ACTION 1
Fill two buckets with lukewarm water, which will be used to wash the *met/metah*.

ACTION 2
The group leader removes the sheet that covers the *met/metah*.

ACTION 3
Recite *Vaya'an Vayomer*, which recounts a vision that came to the prophet Zechariah years after Israel's return to the Holy Land from Babylonia.

IV. *VAYA'AN VAYOMER*: We invoke the mythical context from Zechariah.

> *Kavanah*: God, help us to take the first step in preparing _____ [name of the deceased] for this journey. As we do so, may we be conscious to show this *met/metah* the same dignity that God's angels showed to Joshua in preparing him to be *Kohen Gadol*.

Vaya'an vayomer el ha'omdim l'fanav leimor: "Hasiru hab'gadim hatzo'im me'alav." Vayomer elav: "R'eh he'evarti me'alecha avonecha v'halbeish otcha machalatzot."

וַיַּעַן וַיֹּאמֶר אֶל הָעֹמְדִים לְפָנָיו לֵאמֹר: "הָסִירוּ הַבְּגָדִים הַצֹּאִים מֵעָלָיו." וַיֹּאמֶר אֵלָיו: "רְאֵה הֶעֱבַרְתִּי מֵעָלֶיךָ עֲוֹנֶךָ וְהַלְבֵּשׁ אֹתְךָ מַחֲלָצוֹת."

And he [the angel of God] spoke up and said to his attendants, "Take the filthy garments off him [the High Priest]," and he said to him [the High Priest], "See, I have removed your guilt from you and you shall be clothed in [priestly] robes."

ZECHARIAH 3:4

COMMENTARY

Three times in the liturgy, we recite verses from Zechariah: here, at the beginning of our physical interaction with the body; later, as we prepare to dress the body in priestly garments (see *Sos Asis*—item IX in Chapter 8); and in our final interaction with the *met/metah* (see part XIIIa of *Hineih Mitato* in Chapter 9).

The verse here invokes the precedent set by God's angel, who instructs the accompanying angels to remove the soiled clothes from Joshua, the *Kohen Gadol*. (See the section "Five Underlying Concepts and Settings for *Taharah*" in Chapter 1.) Removing the covering/clothing marks the beginning of the physical cleansing, but it is a step that is part of the process that will also allow the *neshamah* to move on.

Thus, we are implicitly likening the deceased to the High Priest, and, at the same time, likening ourselves to the angels who remove Joshua's clothing. Just as we remove the deceased's soiled covering, we hope that God will remove any spiritual "soiling" from the *met/metah*, and reveal the pure spirit of the *neshamah*.[32]

32. Rabbi Yechezkel Schlingenbaum, *Tahara Guide* (Prepared for the New Haven Chevra Kadisha, 1991) p. 22.

Recitation of this verse also acts as a transition from the preparatory stage to the physical actions of *taharah*.

In some sense, *Vaya'an Vayomer* involves all three of the primary "entities" in the room: *we* who are reciting it; the *met/metah* (by analogy with Joshua); and God, who is the force behind what is happening. In fact, the verse directly involves yet another of our "entities," in that the speaker is actually one of God's angels (as is clear from the preceding verse, Zechariah 3:3).

ACTION 4

The group performs two actions simultaneously:

- **Recite from Song of Songs**: One or more of the *m'taharim* recite *Rosho Ketem Paz* (for a male) or *Hinach Yafah* (for a female). (The verses for a male are traditional, based on *Ma'avar Yabok*; we have selected alternative, parallel verses that might be used for a female.[33])
- **Wash the body**: Others of the *m'taharim* wash the body of the *met/metah* as outlined below. More than one area may be cleaned at a time, as the team works together.
    - Remove items from *met/metah*:
        The leader should look for bandages, tags, or jewelry that are on, but not directly attached to the *met/metah* and remove them if this can be done without tearing the skin. Bandages and tags should be buried with the *met/metah*; jewelry or other valuable items may be given away to others.[34]
    - Wash the body as follows:
        –Wash the head, taking care to keep the eyes, mouth, and nostrils covered.
        –Wash the neck.
        –Wash the right arm, including the hand.
        –Wash the right upper half of the body.
        –Wash the right lower half of the body.
        –Wash the right leg, including the foot.
        –Wash the left arm, including the hand.

---

33. Some have suggested that in the case of a *taharah* of a child, one should choose yet other verses, without the sexual overtones of either *Rosho Ketem Paz* or *Hinach Yafah*.

34. Shulhan Aruch, *Yoreh Deah*, par. 349.2h

—Wash the left upper half of the body.

—Wash the left lower half of the body.

—Wash the left leg, including the foot.

—Incline the body on its left side. Wash the right side of the back in the same order as the right side of the front.

—Incline the body on its right side. Wash the left side of the back in the same order as the left side of the front.

Also:

—Clean under fingernails and toenails with a wooden implement.

—Remove any nail polish.

- Dry *met/metah* and table

  Dry the *met/metah* and the table with sheets or towels. Do not use the same sheet or towel to dry the *met/metah* and the table.

- Cover *met/metah*

  Cover the *met/metah* with a clean sheet.

- Remove gloves

  Remove and discard gloves. (*M'taharim* will put on clean gloves at the start of the next section of the ritual—see ACTION 1 of Chapter 7.)

V. *ROSHO KETEM PAZ* or *HINACH YAFAH*:[35] We praise the body of the *met/metah* as we physically cleanse it.

> *Kavanah:* Just as this *met/metah* was created in God's image, and beautiful while alive, so may we continue to recognize the beauty of his/her *neshamah.*

For a male:

Rosho ketem paz; k'vutzotav taltalim	רֹאשׁוֹ כֶּתֶם פָּז ; קְוֻצּוֹתָיו תַּלְתַּלִּים
sh'chorot ka'orev: Enav k'yonim al	שְׁחֹרוֹת כָּעוֹרֵב : עֵינָיו כְּיוֹנִים עַל
afikei mayim, rochatzot bechalav	אֲפִיקֵי מָיִם, רֹחֲצוֹת בֶּחָלָב

---

35. Some versions of the liturgy pick and choose verses from Chapters 5 and 7 of Song of Songs to match the physical actions more precisely.

yosh'vot al mileit: L'chayav ka'arugat habosem migd'lot merkachim; siftotav shoshanim not'fot mor oveir: Yadav g'lilei zahav m'mula'im batarshish; me'av eshet shen m'ulefet sapirim: Shokav amudei shesh m'yusadim al adnei faz; mar'eihu kalvanon bachur ka'arazim: Chiko mamtakim v'chulo machamadim; zeh dodi v'zeh rei'i b'not yerushalam.

יֹשְׁבוֹת עַל מִלֵּאת : לְחָיָו כַּעֲרוּגַת הַבֹּשֶׂם מִגְדְּלוֹת מֶרְקָחִים ; שִׂפְתוֹתָיו שׁוֹשַׁנִּים נֹטְפוֹת מוֹר עֹבֵר : יָדָיו גְּלִילֵי זָהָב מְמֻלָּאִים בַּתַּרְשִׁישׁ ; מֵעָיו עֶשֶׁת שֵׁן מְעֻלֶּפֶת סַפִּירִים : שׁוֹקָיו עַמּוּדֵי שֵׁשׁ מְיֻסָּדִים עַל אַדְנֵי פָז ; מַרְאֵהוּ כַּלְּבָנוֹן בָּחוּר כָּאֲרָזִים : חִכּוֹ מַמְתַקִּים וְכֻלּוֹ מַחֲמַדִּים ; זֶה דוֹדִי וְזֶה רֵעִי בְּנוֹת יְרוּשָׁלָם.

His head is finest gold; his locks are curled and black as a raven. His eyes are like doves by watercourses, bathed in milk set by a brimming pool. His cheeks are like beds of spices, banks of perfumes. His lips are like lilies; they drip flowing myrrh. His hands are rods of gold, studded with beryl; his belly a tablet of ivory adorned with sapphires. His legs are like marble pillars set in sockets of fine gold; he is majestic as Lebanon, stately as the cedars. His mouth is delicious and all of him is delightful. Such is my beloved; such is my darling, O maidens of Jerusalem.

SONG OF SONGS, 5:11-16

For a female:

Hinach yafah ra'yati hinach yafah; einayich yonim miba'ad l'tzamateich; sa'reich k'eder ha'izim shegalshu meihar gil'ad: Shinayich k'eder haktzuvot she'alu min-harachtzah; shekulam mat'imot v'shakulah ein

הִנָּךְ יָפָה רַעְיָתִי הִנָּךְ יָפָה ; עֵינַיִךְ יוֹנִים מִבַּעַד לְצַמָּתֵךְ ; שַׂעְרֵךְ כְּעֵדֶר הָעִזִּים שֶׁגָּלְשׁוּ מֵהַר גִּלְעָד : שִׁנַּיִךְ כְּעֵדֶר הַקְּצוּבוֹת שֶׁעָלוּ מִן־הָרַחְצָה ; שֶׁכֻּלָּם מַתְאִימוֹת וְשַׁכֻּלָה אֵין

40

bahem: K'chut hashani siftotayich
umidbarech na'veh k'felach harimon
rakateich miba'ad l'tzamateich:
K'migdal David tzava'reich banu'i
l'talpiyot elef hamagen talu'i alav kol
shiltei hagiborim: Shnei shadayich
kishnei afarim t'omei tz'viyah haro'im
bashoshanim: Ad sheyafu'ach hayom
v'nasu hatz'lalim eileich li el har hamor
v'el giv'at hal'vonah: Kulach yafah
ra'yati umum ein bach.

בָּהֶם : כְּחוּט הַשָּׁנִי שִׂפְתֹתַיִךְ
וּמִדְבָּרֵיךְ נָאוֶה כְּפֶלַח הָרִמּוֹן
רַקָּתֵךְ מִבַּעַד לְצַמָּתֵךְ :
כְּמִגְדַּל דָּוִיד צַוָּארֵךְ בָּנוּי
לְתַלְפִּיּוֹת אֶלֶף הַמָּגֵן תָּלוּי עָלָיו כֹּל
שִׁלְטֵי הַגִּבּוֹרִים : שְׁנֵי שָׁדַיִךְ
כִּשְׁנֵי עֳפָרִים תְּאוֹמֵי צְבִיָּה הָרוֹעִים
בַּשּׁוֹשַׁנִּים : עַד שֶׁיָּפוּחַ הַיּוֹם
וְנָסוּ הַצְּלָלִים אֵלֶךְ לִי אֶל־הַר הַמּוֹר
וְאֶל־גִּבְעַת הַלְּבוֹנָה : כֻּלָּךְ יָפָה
רַעְיָתִי וּמוּם אֵין בָּךְ.

Ah, you are fair, my darling, ah, you are fair. Your eyes are like doves behind your veil. Your hair is like a flock of goats streaming down Mount Gilead. Your teeth are like a flock of ewes, climbing up from the washing pool. All of them bear twins, and not one loses her young. Your lips are like a crimson thread, your mouth is lovely, your brow behind your veil like a pomegranate split open. Your neck is like the tower of David, built to hold weapons, hung with a thousand shields—all the quivers of warriors. Your breasts are like two fawns, twins of a gazelle, browsing among the lilies. When the day blows gently and the shadows flee, I will betake me to the mount of myrrh, to the hill of frankincense. Every part of you is fair, my darling, there is no blemish in you.

SONG OF SONGS, 4:1-7

COMMENTARY

Though an allegorical understanding of Song of Songs is possible, Berechiah likely chose these verses because of their physical specificity. Perhaps the subtlety here is that we are contemplating the inner beauty as well as the outer beauty, and one cannot divorce the two. (As a Kabbalist, Berechiah would have been fully aware of this connection.)

Regardless, the liturgy reminds us that every person is *kadosh* and created *b'tzelem Elohim*—in God's image. The praise of the physical body reminds us, the *m'taharim*, that the deceased once was (and perhaps still is) a beautiful human being. (It may even occur to us to hope that someone said something like these sentiments to the *met/metah* while s/he was still alive.)

Rabbi Mosha Epstein connects the individual verses with specific personal attributes, and adds, "These attributes of *Rosho* form the essence of a Jew. In *Rosho* we are saying to the Almighty, have pity on the deceased and spare his [sic] suffering because of the special attributes of a person. Either he (the deceased) possessed all of these marvelous attributes, or he belonged to a Nation that was considered very special because it exemplified these traits and practices."[36]

Epstein also cites a kabbalistic tradition that reciting Song of Songs before Shabbat helps save one from *Gehinom*.[37] This allusion to Shabbat brings to mind the teaching that Shabbat is *me'ein olam haba*—a taste of the future world.

Ma'avar Yabok says, in connection with the recitation of *Rosho*: "The washers shall be mindful, during the washing of each part of the body, of the verse *Hineih mah tov*."[38] (These are the opening words of Psalm 133: "How good and how pleasant it is that brothers [sic] dwell together.")

We (the *m'taharim*) and the *met/metah* (about whom we are speaking) seem to be the main "entities" involved. Of course, God, in whose image both the *met/metah* and we were created, is not far from our awareness.

---

36. Rabbi Mosha Epstein, *Tahara Manual of Practices*, 3rd Edition (Bridgeport, CT: 2005), p. 125. For commentary on the meaning of the specific verses, see p. 124.
37. Epstein, p. 124; cited from *The Complete ArtScroll Siddur* (Brooklyn: 1984), p. 298.
38. See p. 2 of Moss translation (see footnote 1).

CHAPTER SUMMARY

The *Rechitzah* section of the *taharah* ritual appears to have no summary verse or statement; rather, the specific order of washing, by itself, marks the completion of this section. Once the washing is complete, the body and table are dried and the body is covered with a clean sheet.

Chapter 7
The Ritual and the Liturgy: *Taharah*

CHAPTER OVERVIEW

Taharah is the third and core step in the *taharah* ritual and includes the single most essential act – the "purifying" washing of the body through the pouring of water. This act enables us to help the *met/metah* change status. As noted earlier, the word *taharah* is often used to refer to just this act alone.

Taharah proceeds as follows:
- Recite *Amar Rabbi Akiva,* which combines a Mishnaic passage with quotations from Song of Songs, Isaiah, and Ezekiel.
- Pour water on the *met/metah,* while reciting the phrase *tahor hu/ t'horah hi.* This is the central element in the entire ritual, both in the sense that it is the core element, and because it is the middle element of the middle section of the ritual.
- Recite a concluding phrase, which is an adaptation of Leviticus 11:44.

ACTION 1

Before beginning the *taharah* section, do the following preparatory steps in sequence. (If preferred, these steps can be done after reciting *Amar Rabbi Akiva.*)

- **Wash hands:** This is done without a *brachah.* See ACTION 1 at the start of Chapter 5 for details on the handwashing process.
- **Re-glove:** Put on a new pair of gloves.
- **Prepare buckets:** Fill three full buckets of cold, fresh water. Each bucket should contain approximately 8 quarts, or 3 *kavim.*
- **Immerse and arrange two-by-fours:** Dunk each end of the four varnished wooden two-by-fours in the water. Carefully place the four varnished wooden two-by-fours under the body of the *met/metah* at the ankles, thighs, lower back, and shoulders.

⟡ Guidelines for pouring water

The *m'taharim* should be familiar with the following guidelines for pouring water in the "purification" step of the ritual, which occurs after reciting *Amar Rabbi Akiva.*

Three members should pour the water over the *met/metah* in succession with no interruption in the flow. One team member should pour the first bucket of water over the *met/metah*, and before all the water has been emptied, a second team member should begin pouring the second bucket of water over the *met/metah*, continuing from where the first pourer ends, so that their pouring overlaps. Before the second bucket of water has been emptied, a third team member should begin pouring the third bucket of water over the *met/metah*. If there is any interruption in the pouring, members should refill their buckets and repeat the process.

The water is poured from head to foot in a counterclockwise motion. Beginning on the front side of the *met/metah,* pour the water down the right side of the body and up the left, taking care not to get water in the mouth, eyes, or nostrils of the *met/metah.*

ACTION 2
Recite *Amar Rabbi Akiva.*

VI. *AMAR RABBI AKIVA:* The reasons for the pouring of water

> *Kavanah:* Help us prepare this *neshamah* to
> enter the heavenly kingdom and to witness
> Your Presence.

Amar Rabbi Akiva: Ashreichem	אָמַר רַבִּי עֲקִיבָא : אַשְׁרֵיכֶם
Yisra'el, lifnei mi atem mitaharin	יִשְׂרָאֵל, לִפְנֵי מִי אַתֶּם מִטַּהֲרִין
umi m'taher etchem? Avichem	וּמִי מְטַהֵר אֶתְכֶם ? אֲבִיכֶם
shebashamayim, shene'emar: "V'zarakti	שֶׁבַּשָּׁמַיִם, שֶׁנֶּאֱמַר : "וְזָרַקְתִּי
alechem mayim t'horim ut'hartem."	עֲלֵיכֶם מַיִם טְהוֹרִים וּטְהַרְתֶּם"
V'omer: "Mikveh	(יחזקאל לו:כה). וְאוֹמֵר : "מִקְוֵה
Yisra'el Adonai." Ma mikveh	יִשְׂרָאֵל יְיָ" (ירמיה יז:יג). מַה מִקְוֶה
m'taher et hat'me'im, af haKadosh	מְטַהֵר אֶת הַטְּמֵאִים, אַף הַקָּדוֹשׁ
Baruch Hu m'taher et Yisra'el.	בָּרוּךְ הוּא מְטַהֵר אֶת יִשְׂרָאֵל.

Rabbi Akiva said: You are fortunate, Israel. Before whom do you purify yourselves and who purifies you? Your God in heaven. As it is said: "I will sprinkle clean water upon you and you shall be clean..." (EZEKIEL 36:25). And it says: "O hope [*mikveh*] of Israel! O Adonai" (JEREMIAH 17:13). Just as the ritual bath [*mikveh*[39]] purifies the impure, so does the Holy One, blessed be He, purify Israel.

MISHNAH YOMA 8:9

Ma'ayan ganim b'er mayim chayim

v'nozlim min l'vanon.

מַעְיַן גַּנִּים בְּאֵר מַיִם חַיִּים
וְנֹזְלִים מִן לְבָנוֹן.

You are a garden spring, a well of fresh water, a rill of Lebanon.

SONG OF SONGS 4:15

Im rachatz Adonai et tzo'at b'not

tziyon v'et d'mei Y'rushalayim yadi'ach

mikirbah b'ru'ach mishpat uv'ru'ach

ba'eir.

אִם רָחַץ אֲדֹנָי אֵת צֹאַת בְּנוֹת
צִיּוֹן וְאֵת דְּמֵי יְרוּשָׁלַיִם יָדִיחַ
מִקִּרְבָּהּ בְּרוּחַ מִשְׁפָּט וּבְרוּחַ
בָּעֵר.

When Adonai has washed away the filth of the daughters of Zion, and from Jerusalem's midst has rinsed out her infamy – in a spirit of judgment and in a spirit of purging.

ISAIAH 4:4

---

39. In its use within English, the Hebrew word for a ritual bath is usually transliterated as *mikvah*—accented on the first syllable—but this reflects the common Ashkenazi pronunciation. This word is identical with the word in the phrase cited from Jeremiah, and is more accurately transliterated, based on the standard Sephardic pronunciation, as *mikveh*—with the accent on the second syllable. So we are using the transliteration *mikveh* throughout.

V'zarakti aleichem mayim t'horim
ut'hartem mikol tum'otechem umikol
giluleichem ataheir etchem.

וְזָרַקְתִּי עֲלֵיכֶם מַיִם טְהוֹרִים
וּטְהַרְתֶּם מִכֹּל טֻמְאוֹתֵיכֶם וּמִכָּל
גִּלּוּלֵיכֶם אֲטַהֵר אֶתְכֶם.

I will sprinkle clean water upon you, and you shall
be clean: I will cleanse you from all from all your
uncleanness and from all your fetishes.

EZEKIEL 36:25

COMMENTARY

In many religions, water has the power to transform status,
and it plays that very role in our ritual, transforming the
deceased from being *tamei* to being *tahor*. (See the discussion
of these terms in the section "Five Underlying Concepts and
Settings for *Taharah*" in Chapter 1.)

Amar Rabbi Akiva combines a citation from Mishnah with
several Biblical verses. The key element of this prayer is
Ezekiel 36:25, which makes a clear connection between this
change of status and the pouring of water. So vital is this verse
that it occurs twice here: at the beginning (in part), within
the Mishnaic citation, and at the end (in full), perhaps for
emphasis. (Or maybe it is repeated in full at the end simply
because the Mishnah itself quoted only part of the verse.)

The Hebrew root *tet-hei-resh* (the root of *tahor*) appears twice
in the (partial) Ezekiel verse, four other times within the
Mishnaic citation, plus three more times when the full verse
from Ezekiel is cited. *Amar Rabbi Akiva* also contains repeated
references to water, pouring, and washing (at least eight
distinct references). Thus, this prayer gives a powerful message
that the water that we are about to pour has the effect of
transforming the status of the deceased. But lest we overstate
our own role, the quotations indicate quite clearly that it is
God who is making this transformation happen. In Ezekiel's
verse, the "I" of "I will sprinkle" and "I will cleanse" is clearly
God. Similarly, in the verse from Isaiah, we have "When

48

Adonai has washed away the filth…." Thus, when we, the *m'taharim*, pour water, we are simply acting as God's agents.

Further comments:
- There is a delightful wordplay in the Mishnaic passage. Rabbi Akiva quotes Jeremiah, who describes God as the *mikveh* of Israel. In Jeremiah's context, *mikveh* clearly has the meaning of "hope." But the word also means a ritual bath (which can make both people and objects *tahor*), and Akiva plays on this dual meaning to say that God, who is our *mikveh* in the sense of "hope," will also be our *mikveh* in the sense of "an entity that 'purifies'." In some communities, the *m'taharim* immerse the *met/metah* in a *mikveh* rather than laying the body on the table and pouring water over it (or standing the body up and pouring water over it).
- The verse from Song of Songs was perhaps chosen because it fits the "water" theme of *Amar Rabbi Akiva*.
- The verse from Isaiah continues the "water" theme. Its message, though, is rather harsh, and perhaps the verse from Ezekiel was repeated at the end to soften the tone of the Isaiah verse.

ACTION 3
- If needed, review who will pour the first, second, and third bucket of water.
- Uncover the *met/metah completely.*
- Pour the three buckets of water over the *met/metah*, following the guidelines at the beginning of this chapter, while chanting *Tahor hu/T'horah Hi* throughout the pouring.

VII. *TAHOR HU/T'HORAH HI:* The actual moment of transformation

[No *kavanah* is needed for this two-word chant. It is the one portion of the liturgy that virtually every member of a *Chevra Kadisha* understands.]

49

For a male:

Tahor hu.

טָהוֹר הוּא.

He is pure.

For a female:

T'horah hi.

טְהוֹרָה הִיא.

She is pure.

COMMENTARY

The uninterrupted pouring of water over the body marks the physical moment of transformation; the chanted, formulaic recitation of the words *tahor hu/t'horah hi* marks the sealing of the event. Thus, whether or not the words have literal meaning in transforming the *met/metah*, they serve as a chanted stamp of conclusion to the entire process. This declaration "makes it so," just like "I now pronounce you man and wife" in a wedding.

ACTION 4

Recite *V'hitkadashtem* three times, expressing the completion of this stage of the ritual.

VIII. *V'HITKADASHTEM:* The closing of the ritual of *taharah*

Kavanah: By pouring of the water, we have completed the process of *taharah*.

[The words below are recited three times.]

V'hitkadishtem vih'yitem k'doshim ki

kadosh ani Adonai.

וְהִתְקַדִּשְׁתֶּם וִהְיִיתֶם קְדֹשִׁים כִּי
קָדוֹשׁ אֲנִי יהוה.

50

You shall sanctify yourselves and be holy, for I, Adonai, am holy.

BASED ON LEVITICUS 11:44[40]

COMMENTARY

What is now needed is a final, almost triumphant proclamation of all that the *m'taharim* have done, affirming that the key task has been performed properly. Subtly, we also proclaim that the *taharah* ritual is Torah-based.

This verse, with its threefold repetition of the root *kuf-dalet-shin* (the root of *kadosh*—holy), and the fact that the verse itself contains seven words (a symbol of completeness), plus its recitation by the *m'taharim* three times (another symbol of completeness), is almost an overstatement of conclusion! For sure, we have done all that we have needed to do, the transformation is complete and we can now say for certain that the *neshamah* is *tahor/t'horah*.

Comment: It would have been easy to lose sight of the hallowed nature of what we are doing at this point, because the pouring of water can lead to a mess on the floor and a bunch of mopping to do, not to mention putting away the buckets and boards. So the repetition of this verse is as much for the *m'taharim* as it is for the *met/metah*. Therefore, it is helpful that the liturgy gives us repeated occurrences of the root for holiness.

ACTION 5

- **Dry *met/metah*, etc.:** Dry the *met/metah*, the two-by-fours, and the table using sheets or towels. Do not use the same sheet or towel to dry the *met/metah* that is used on the boards or table.
- **Remove boards:** Remove the boards and place them aside. Cover the *met/metah* with a clean sheet.

---

40. The first six Hebrew words here appear in the middle of Leviticus 11:44. The final "*Adonai*" here does occur in the verse but not following these six words. (The whole phrase "*Ki kadosh Ani Adonai*" does occur elsewhere in Leviticus.) The final "*Adonai*" was perhaps included at the end here so the verse would have seven words, a symbol of completion.

CHAPTER SUMMARY

We have completed the key step of the entire ritual—the *taharah* pouring within the *taharah* section of the overall *taharah* ritual—and can now declare that the *met/metah* is *tahor/t'horah*.

Chapter 8
The Ritual and the Liturgy:
Halbashah and *Halanah*

CHAPTER OVERVIEW

Now that we have cleaned the body of the *met/metah* and proclaimed it (and the *neshamah*) *tahor/t'horah*, we are ready to assist this soul along the next step of the journey. The fourth step in the *taharah* ritual is dressing the *met/metah* and placing him or her in the *aron*.

Following Zechariah's vision, we clothe the *met/metah* in *tachrichim*, white burial garments, recalling those worn by the ancient *Kohen Gadol* when entering the Holy of Holies. During *halbashah*, the *met/metah* is compared to and addressed as the *Kohen Gadol*.[41] In *halanah*, we place the body in its "vehicle"—the *aron*—for travel. The liturgy reflects these two major elements of the ritual.

This chapter provides information about *halachic* burial clothing, as well as the order and manner of dressing the *met/metah*.

ACTION 1

Recite *Sos Asis,* which consists of verses from Isaiah and Zechariah.

> **IX. SOS ASIS: We prepare to dress the *met/metah* in priestly/ spiritual garments.**

>> *Kavanah*: We stand here having completed the pouring ritual of *taharah*, preparing to dress this *met/metah* in plain linen garments, like the simple linens worn by the *Kohen Gadol* who served in the Temple.

---

41. For a fuller discussion of the role of the image of the *Kohen Gadol,* see "Five Underlying Concepts and Settings for *Taharah*" in Chapter 1.

Sos asis ba'Adonai tageil nafshi
beilohai ki hilbishani bigdei yesha
m'il tzedakah y'atani kechatan
y'chahein p'eir v'chakalah ta'deh
cheilehah.

שׂוֹשׂ אָשִׂישׂ בַּיהוה תָּגֵל נַפְשִׁי
בֵּאלֹהַי כִּי הִלְבִּישַׁנִי בִּגְדֵי יֶשַׁע
מְעִיל צְדָקָה יְעָטָנִי כֶּחָתָן
יְכַהֵן פְּאֵר וְכַכַּלָּה תַּעְדֶּה
כֵּלֶיהָ.

I greatly rejoice in Adonai, my whole being exults
in my God. For God has clothed me with garments
of triumph; wrapped me in a robe of victory, like
a bridegroom adorned with a turban, like a bride
bedecked with her finery.

ISAIAH 61:10

Va'omar: "Yasimu tzanif tahor al
rosho." Vayasimu hatzanif hatahor al
rosho vayalbishuhu b'gadim umal'ach
Adonai omed.

וָאֹמַר: "יָשִׂימוּ צָנִיף טָהוֹר עַל
רֹאשׁוֹ." וַיָּשִׂימוּ הַצָּנִיף הַטָּהוֹר עַל
רֹאשׁוֹ וַיַּלְבִּשֻׁהוּ בְּגָדִים וּמַלְאַךְ
יהוה עֹמֵד.

Then he gave the order, "Let a pure diadem be placed
on his head." And they placed the pure diadem on his
head, and they clothed him in [priestly] garments, as
the angel of Adonai stood by.

ZECHARIAH 3:5

Ki cha'aretz totzi tzimchah uch'ganah
zeiru'eha tatzmi'ach ken Adonai
Elohim yatzmi'ach tzedakah ut'hilah
neged kol hagoyim.

כִּי כָאָרֶץ תּוֹצִיא צִמְחָה וּכְגַנָּה
זֵרוּעֶיהָ תַצְמִיחַ כֵּן אֲדֹנָי
יהוה יַצְמִיחַ צְדָקָה וּתְהִלָּה
נֶגֶד כָּל הַגּוֹיִם.

For the earth brings forth her growth, and a garden
makes the seed shoot up, so Adonai, God, will make
victory and renown shoot up in the presence of all the
nations.

ISAIAH 61:11

V'nachacha Adonai tamid v'hisbi'a

b'tzachtzachot nafshecha v'atzmotecha

yachalitz v'hayita k'gan raveh

uch'motza mayim asher lo y'chaz'vu

meimav.

וְנָחֲךָ יהוה תָּמִיד וְהִשְׂבִּיעַ
בְּצַחְצָחוֹת נַפְשֶׁךָ וְעַצְמֹתֶיךָ
יַחֲלִיץ וְהָיִיתָ כְּגַן רָוֶה
וּכְמוֹצָא מַיִם אֲשֶׁר לֹא יְכַזְּבוּ
מֵימָיו.

And Adonai will guide you always; God will slake
your thirst in parched places and give strength to your
bones. You shall be like a watered garden, like a spring
whose waters do not fail.

ISAIAH 58:11

COMMENTARY

Verses from Isaiah surround a verse from Zechariah, and we
combine two motifs: that of the *Kohen Gadol* (implicit in
Zechariah and referenced in the first Isaiah verse: "adorned
with a turban") and that of a bride and groom (explicit in the
first Isaiah verse). It seems fitting that these images be blended
here, for the *Kohen Gadol* and a couple at their wedding are
all engaged in status transformation.

In Zechariah, we continue with his vision of Joshua. After
seeing that Joshua is now dressed in fine garments, Zechariah
intercedes in his own vision and asks that the office of the
Kohen Gadol be restored to Joshua, and that he be dressed
in the full regalia of the *Kohen Gadol*.[42] This latter action is
precisely what we are getting ready to do for the *met/metah*.
We also see here another appearance by the angel of God
(whom we may imagine to be in the room with us).

The verses from Isaiah speak of the wonderful things we will
experience upon our return to the homeland. This is our
wish for the *neshamah* as well. The Isaiah verses also provide
images of nature and rebirth, which are especially suitable for
the occasion that marks both the "return to dust" of the body

42. Schlingenbaum, p. 23.

55

and, at least in some sense, the rebirth of the *neshamah*, or, at least, its potential "birth" into the next world.

Linguistically, the opening phrase *sos asis* here conjures up the nearly identical phrase *sos tasis* from the *Sheva Brachot* of the wedding ceremony.[43] This echo is combined with flashbacks to *tahor* and *mayim* from earlier parts of this liturgy, and all are now encased in a framework of *tzedakah*: *m'il tzedakah y'atani* in Isaiah 61:10 (translated above as "wrapped me in a robe of victory"), and *yatzmi'ach tzedakah* in Isaiah 61:11 (translated above as "will make victory and renown shoot up"). Speaking of robes: the wedding reference calls to mind the *kittel*—the wedding garment that may someday become the last part of the *tachrichim*.

Perhaps these references to *tzedakah* call forth another phrase in the back of the mind, *tzedakah tatzil mimavet*[44] ("*tzedakah* saves from death"), which touches the very essence of the entire ritual. *Tzedakah,* conceived of as "that which we are obligated to do during our life," is here transformed into an act that the *Chevra Kadisha* performs in order to honor the soul that has just died. In a way, this act of *tzedakah*— understood now as "obligation"—reminds us of how the *neshamah* lived and of how we should live, an appropriate message even to those *m'taharim* in the room who may need spiritual sustenance. And this may be a further reason why the tradition exists to give *tzedakah* in memory of someone who has died.

ACTION 2
Prepare the *tachrichim* for placing on the *met/metah*.

◯ General background and information about *tachrichim*
The *m'taharim* should be familiar with all parts of the *tachrichim* (burial clothing) before they begin to dress the *met/metah*. Consult the following list, then lay out the *tachrichim* and make sure they are all clean and unstained.

---

43. The text of the *Sheva Brachot* appears in the Babylonian Talmud, *Ketubot* 8a.
44. Proverbs 10:2.

Men's and women's *tachrichim* differ slightly. Where a significant difference exists, we specify what is for a man and what is for a woman.

- *Mitznefet*:
  —For a male: The *mitznefet* is a headdress that should fit over the head of the *met*, covering his entire face and the back of his head to the neck.
  —For a female: A woman's headdress has two parts: a bonnet to cover her hair and a face cover or apron to cover her face.
- *Michnasayim* (male and female): These are trousers that have the pant legs sewn shut at the feet. *Michnasayim* are fastened at the waist with a long band.
- *K'tonet* (male and female): A *k'tonet* is a large shirt or blouse. It has sleeves and reaches to the waist.
- *Kittel* (male and female): The *kittel* is a long robe with sleeves and a collar. It may pull over the head, or it may open down the front. A *kittel* usually reaches the thighs or knees. If the *met/metah* owned a *kittel,* he or she may be buried in it.
- *Avnet* (male and female): An *avnet* is a sash or belt. It is placed over the *kittel* and wrapped around the body of the *met/metah*.
- *Tallit*:
  —For a male: The *met* is buried wearing a *tallit*, perhaps one worn during his lifetime.
  —For a female: If the *metah* wore a *tallit* during her lifetime, she should be buried in one, preferably one she owned and wore. If the *metah* did not wear a *tallit* during her lifetime, she is not buried in one.
  —For both male and female: A *tallit* used in burial should have all ornaments removed from it.
  —Regarding children: Only children age 13 and over are buried in a *tallit*; children under 13 are not buried in a *tallit*.
- Apron (female only): Women's *tachrichim* kits typically include an apron that is worn over the *kittel*. A *metah* buried in a *tallit* will not wear an apron.
- *Sovev* (male and female): The final piece of burial garb is the *sovev*, or sheet. It is placed in the *aron* before putting the body in, and is used to encircle the entire body of the *met/metah*.

ACTION 3

Dress the *met/metah* in the order presented below, while reciting the appropriate phrases from *K'tonet Bad Kodesh Yilbash*, etc. This recitation is primarily Leviticus 16:4, which describes the priestly array and makes the comparison of the *met/metah* to the high priest explicit, and also includes Genesis 43:14.

X. *K'TONET BAD KODESH YILBASH*, etc.: We do the actual dressing of the *met/metah*.

[Although the order of the dressing varies slightly among different *Chevra Kadisha* groups, the model for all is the first half of Leviticus 16:4, which describes the attire of the *Kohen Gadol* on Yom Kippur. The second half of Leviticus 16:4, and the verse here from Genesis, are then recited after the dressing is completed.]

> *Kavanah*: As we dress this *met/metah,* let us be conscious that we are clothing him/her in the garments of the *Kohen Gadol.*

[As each item of clothing is put on the *met/metah,* the *m'taharim* recite the appropriate phrase from the first half of the verse. This first half is shown here in its entirety, and then appears below, phrase by phrase, in steps d, c, f, and then b, in accordance with our order of dressing.]

K'tonet bad kodesh yilbash umichn'sei   כְּתֹנֶת בַּד קֹדֶשׁ יִלְבָּשׁ וּמִכְנְסֵי

vad yihyu al b'saro uv'avnet bad   בַד יִהְיוּ עַל בְּשָׂרוֹ וּבְאַבְנֵט בַּד

yachgor uv'mitznefet bad yitznof.   יַחְגֹּר וּבְמִצְנֶפֶת בַּד יִצְנֹף.

> Be dressed in a sacral linen tunic, with linen breeches next to the flesh, and be girt with a linen sash, and wear a linen turban.
>
> LEVITICUS 16:4A

Order of dressing and accompanying phrases

a. *Kippah*:
- For a male: Place a *kippah* on the *met*.
- For a female: Place a *kippah* on the *metah* if she wore one during her lifetime.

b. *Mitznefet:*
- For a male: Fit the *mitznefet* over the head, making sure the face and back of the head are covered.
- For a female: Gather the *metah's* hair loosely off her face. Place the bonnet on the *metah* so that it covers all her hair and the back of her head. Tie the bonnet with a bow or using the method specified for the *michnasayim* (see step c).

As step b is done, recite:

Uv'mitznefet bad yitznof

וּבְמִצְנֶפֶת בַּד יִצְנֹף

and wear a linen turban.

FROM LEVITICUS 16:4A

c. *Michnasayim* (male and female):
- Put the *michnasayim* on the *met/metah*. Two *m'taharim* then tie the sash at the waist. Each takes one end of the tie, and the two twist the ends four times while counting aloud "*alef* (one), *bet* (two), *gimel* (three), *dalet* (four)." Secure the tie with a bow or two slip-knots so that two loops face the head of the *met/metah*. (See diagram in Appendix 4 for tying of knots.)
- For a male: Tie a band around each of the *met's* legs, just above the ankle. One member should tie the band on the right leg, and another member should follow with the left. Tie the bands in the same fashion the *michnasayim* were tied.
- For a female: Tie a band around each of the *metah's* legs, just below the knee. One member should tie the band on the right leg, and another member should follow with the left. Tie the bands in the same fashion the *michnasayim* were tied.

As step c is done, recite:

Umichn'sei vad yihyu al b'saro

וּמִכְנְסֵי בַד יִהְיוּ עַל בְּשָׂרוֹ

with linen breeches next to the flesh

FROM LEVITICUS 16:4A

d. *K'tonet* (male and female):

Dress the *met/metah* in the *k'tonet*. Begin by slipping the sleeves over the arms of the *met/metah* and then pull the body of the *k'tonet* over his or her head. Finish by pulling the *k'tonet* down as far as it stretches. Two people tie the bands at the neck of the *k'tonet* in the same fashion the *michnasayim* were tied. As step 4 is done, recite:

K'tonet bad kodesh yilbash

כְּתֹנֶת בַּד קֹדֶשׁ יִלְבָּשׁ

Be dressed in a sacral linen tunic

FROM LEVITICUS 16:4A

e. *Kittel:* (male and female)

Dress the *met/metah* in the *kittel*. Put the *kittel* on the *met/metah* and tie the bands on the neck in the same fashion as for the *k'tonet*.

f. *Avnet* (male and female):

Wind the *avnet* around the body over the *kittel*. As step 6 is done, recite:

Uv'avnet bad yachgor

וּבְאַבְנֵט בַּד יַחְגֹּר

and be girt with a linen sash

FROM LEVITICUS 16:4A

g. Apron and face cover (for a female only):

If the *metah* will not be buried in a *tallit*, place the apron on her and tuck it into the *avnet*. Next, put the face cover on the *metah*.

h. Recite the second half of Leviticus 16:4, followed by Genesis 43:14:

Bigdei kodesh hem v'rachatz bamayim

et b'saro ul'vasham.

בִּגְדֵי קֹדֶשׁ הֵם וְרָחַץ בַּמַּיִם

אֶת בְּשָׂרוֹ וּלְבֵשָׁם.

They are sacral vestments; and bathe the body in water and then put them on.

LEVITICUS 16:4B

V'El Shaddai yiten lachem rachamim.

וְאֵל שַׁדַּי יִתֵּן לָכֶם רַחֲמִים.

And may El Shaddai give mercy toward you.

GENESIS 43:14

COMMENTARY

Each of the opening phrases from Leviticus requires us to raise the banal act of dressing to a higher plane of consciousness, so that we are not merely clothing the body, but dressing it in accordance with the divine images from the verses we have seen earlier from Song of Songs and Zechariah. How can we prevent loss of focus while dressing the *neshamah*? The verses here are parallel in function to those of *Rosho Ketem Paz* (or its corresponding prayer for women; for both, see item V in Chapter 6)—that is, they remind us how special this *met/metah* is, and how important our task is.

The final phrase from Leviticus provides us with more water imagery. Although the verse says that "he" [sic] shall bathe "his" flesh, in this case it is *we* who need to do this task, because the *met/metah* is unable to do it.

The concluding verse here, from Genesis, recited while the final knot is being tied, echoes thematically ideas we have seen earlier—about God (here called *El Shaddai*) and *rachamim* (think back to *Chamol*), and serves to conclude the actual dressing of the *met/metah*. This verse functions as a final salutation of the dead— "Go on your way"—after the preparation and dressing of the body has been accomplished.

The liturgy from *Ma'avar Yabok* includes an additional verse from Song of Songs (4:14), describing a set of spices that are even today used in the Sephardic ritual. We might speculate that these were placed in the *aron* with the *met/metah* (perhaps intermingled with the garments), as a way of disguising the unpleasant odors from the body in that pre-refrigeration time. Or perhaps the herbs were ones that were used for healing.

ACTION 4

Actions 4, 5, and 6 comprise the process of placing the *met/metah* in the *aron*, together with several related actions involving the set-up of the *aron*. The initial steps are as follows:

a. Sprinkle some *afar* (soil) from Israel in the *aron*.

b. Place the *sovev* in the *aron* diagonally so that it overlaps the *aron*'s sides.

c. Drape the *tallit* (if one is being used) in the *aron*. Cut off one fringe from the *tallit* and tuck the fringe into the *avnet*. (We cut off the fringe because we do not bury a usable ritual object.)

d. Place the *met/metah* in the *aron*. Make sure that the feet are at the same end as the *Magen David*. *Note:* If there is no *Magen David* on the *aron*, affix one with glue at the foot of the *aron*. At the cemetery, the *Magen David* indicates the feet of the *met/metah* which traditionally point in the direction of Jerusalem.

e. Recite *V'lo Yavo'u*.

XI. *V'LO YAVO'U:* We place the *met/metah* into the *aron*.

> *Kavanah:* We stand here at a liminal, potentially dangerous moment. Help us now as we gently lift the *met/metah* and place him/ her into the *aron*.

[The following verse is recited as we perform our final physical act with the *met/metah:* placing him/her in the *aron*.]

V'lo yavo'u lirot k'vala et hakodesh

vametu.

וְלֹא יָבֹאוּ לִרְאוֹת כְּבַלַּע אֶת הַקֹּדֶשׁ
וָמֵתוּ.

> But let not [the Kohathites] go inside and witness the dismantling of the sanctuary, lest they die.
>
> NUMBERS 4:20

COMMENTARY

In its original context, this verse is a warning to the Kohathites (a branch of the Levite tribe) not to go inside the Temple and witness the dismantling or covering[45] of the holy objects until Aaron and his sons were finished with their work. Were the body we are handling a living being, he/she would be *kadosh*—holy—like those objects in the book of Numbers, and, as a personification of the *Kohen Gadol*, would represent the closest we might come to God and yet still remain alive. As we place the *met/metah* into the *aron*—and are about to "cover" it—we are thus in danger of putting ourselves at risk of death. Hence, the verse comes to remind us of the potential power inherent in the very act of placing someone in an *aron* (here used with the distinct intent of echoing the holy *Aron*, which just by touching it, could cause death).

The verse may also be a warning against looking within the *aron* after our work is done. Once we close the *aron*, it remains closed.

Ma'avar Yabok describes the placing of the dead in the *aron* as a means to "hide the body from the forces of judgment."[46] Berechiah also recommends that this verse be said "in a loud voice" if the deceased is "a distinguished person." Perhaps this is done to warn off those "forces of judgment."

ACTION 5

Continue the activities connected with the *aron*. The next steps are as follows:

a. (optional) Place pieces of broken pottery (shards) on the eyelids and mouth of the *met/metah*. Placing of the shards was, we speculate, a practice from ancient times when earth from the land of Israel was not available, so earthenware shards were used to remind us of the return to the earth.

b. Place *afar* from Israel on the eyes, heart, and genitals of the *met/metah*. Be careful to keep the *afar* out of the nose and mouth.

c. Recite *V'chiper Admato*.

---

45. Rashi on Numbers 4:20.
46. See p. 5 of Moss translation (see footnote 1).

XII. *V'CHIPER ADMATO*: We place shards (where practiced) and *afar* (earth) from Israel on the body of the deceased.

Kavanah: As no one is so righteous as to
have never sinned, we pray for atonement for
_____ [name of the deceased].

V'chiper admato amo.

וְכִפֶּר אַדְמָתוֹ עַמּוֹ.

And cleanse the land of God's people.

DEUTERONOMY 32:43

COMMENTARY

What is the role of earth in this stage of the ritual? In its context in Deuteronomy, the verse apparently meant that God was cleansing the land. But it can also be translated as "And God's land will atone for God's people." In this reading, the verse seems to suggest that earth atones [*kaper*, which has the same root as *v'chiper*] for people. Land cleanses the person by conferring atonement on people. Genesis 3:17-19 indicates that Adam is cursed and has to work the land [*adamah*] to get food, as opposed to just receiving food. This remains the human condition until Adam is returned to the earth [*afar*] at which time the curse is lifted.[47]

ACTION 6

Complete the activities connected with the *aron* with these steps:

a. Wrap the *tallit* over the *met/metah*, first over the left side and then over the right.

b. Wrap the *sovev* over the *met/metah*. Begin with the feet, then proceed to wrap the right side of the body, the left side of the body, and the head.

c. Place any items that must be buried with the *met/metah* at the foot of the *aron*. These items include loose hairs, false teeth, and blood-stained clothing.

---

47. Our thanks to Alison Jordan for assistance in understanding this component of the liturgy.

Note: The closing of the *aron* is included in this book as part of the Concluding Prayers, following the closing *Mechilah* (see Chapter 9).

CHAPTER SUMMARY

By completing the dressing of the *met/metah* symbolically in the garments of the *Kohen Gadol,* we are taking the next step in readying him or her for the next step on his/her journey.

Chapter 9
The Ritual and the Liturgy: Concluding Prayers

CHAPTER OVERVIEW
Our physical activity with the *met/metah* is done. The ritual concludes with a series of prayers, primarily "protective" in nature, as well as a final, personal statement to the *met/metah* from the *m'taharim*, and then the *aron* is closed and moved out of the *taharah* room.

ACTION 1
Recite *Hineih Mitato*. The rubric of *Hineih Mitato* encompasses a collection of verses from several sources. Though they form a unified whole, it seems helpful to list them here in three distinct parts.

XIII. *HINEIH MITATO:* We invoke various protections from "terror by night."

> *Kavanah*: We pray that God, in the image of Solomon's mighty men, will protect
> _____ [name of the deceased].

XIIIa. SOLOMON'S MIGHTY WARRIORS: Their swords are ready.

Hineih mitato sheliShlomo shishim	הִנֵּה מִטָּתוֹ שֶׁלִּשְׁלֹמֹה שִׁשִּׁים
giborim saviv lah migiborei Yisra'el:	גִּבֹּרִים סָבִיב לָהּ מִגִּבֹּרֵי יִשְׂרָאֵל:
Kulam achuzei cherev m'lumdei	כֻּלָּם אֲחֻזֵי חֶרֶב מְלֻמְּדֵי
milchamah ish charbo al y'recho	מִלְחָמָה אִישׁ חַרְבּוֹ עַל יְרֵכוֹ
mipachad baleilot.	מִפַּחַד בַּלֵּילוֹת.

> There is Solomon's couch, encircled by sixty warriors of the warriors of Israel, all of them trained in warfare, skilled in battle, each with sword on thigh because of terror by night.
>
> Song of Songs 3:7-8

67

COMMENTARY

We note, first, that the word *mitato,* translated here as "[Solomon's] couch," is more properly understood as "bier"— that is, the base on which the deceased is carried. The verses are speaking of Solomon's funeral.

But the most powerful image from these verses is the one at the end: "terror by night" (literally, "nights"). Throughout this ritual, we have been aware of dangers, both physical and spiritual. For many of us, darkness suggests peril, instability, and lack of control. We might feel alone, afraid, and powerless. We now name that fear, and "terror by night" becomes a frightful description of the terror we have been feeling and that now lies ahead (at least for the *met/metah*). These two verses heighten our awareness that the *neshamah* is about to embark (indeed, has already embarked!) on a journey to the unknown. And of course, the body also has a journey ahead.

But we do not send him/her off unprotected. We liken the deceased here to Solomon, with the *aron* in the role of the "couch." As royalty, Solomon (and hence our deceased) is surrounded by "60 warriors," each of whom is well versed in the skills of warfare and holds a sword on his thigh. This sounds like good protection. And perhaps this image was also intended to refer to the pallbearers.

It may be that the verse is also intended as comfort to the *m'taharim,* assuring them that they have completed their part in the ritual and that "others" (the warriors) will take over the care of the *met/metah* from here on.

We might also note a linguistic echo: the warriors *saviv* ("surround") Solomon's couch, reminding us of the final garment, the *sovev,* with which we wrap the *met/metah* in the *aron.*

XIIIb. *Y'VARECH'CHA:* We pronounce the *Birkat Kohanim* (Priestly Blessing).

For a male:

Y'varech'cha Adonai v'yishm'recha:

Ya'eir Adonai panav eilecha vichuneka:

Yisa Adonai panav eilecha v'yaseim

l'cha shalom.

יְבָרֶכְךָ יהוה וְיִשְׁמְרֶךָ:

יָאֵר יהוה פָּנָיו אֵלֶיךָ וִיחֻנֶּךָּ:

יִשָּׂא יהוה פָּנָיו אֵלֶיךָ וְיָשֵׂם

לְךָ שָׁלוֹם.

May Adonai bless you and protect you.
May Adonai deal kindly and graciously with you.
May Adonai bestow favor upon you and grant you
peace.

NUMBERS 6: 24-26

For a female:

Y'varcheich Adonai v'yishm'reich:

Ya'eir Adonai panav eilayich vichuneich:

Yisa Adonai panav eilayich v'yaseim

lach shalom.

יְבָרְכֵךְ יהוה וְיִשְׁמְרֵךְ:

יָאֵר יהוה פָּנָיו אֵלַיִךְ וִיחֻנֵּךְ:

יִשָּׂא יהוה פָּנָיו אֵלַיִךְ וְיָשֵׂם

לָךְ שָׁלוֹם.

May Adonai bless you and protect you.
May Adonai deal kindly and graciously with you.
May Adonai bestow favor upon you and grant you
peace.

NUMBERS 6: 24-26

COMMENTARY

A plea for a blessing. Not just a quotation about protection, *Birkat Kohanim* is a positive, forward-looking citation, a prayer we use throughout life as a way of asking God for blessing. We intone it here with great reverence as the final time that we can ask for God's blessing on this *neshamah*.

The gradually ascending number of words in each line—3, 5, and 7—create an increasing crescendo of dramatic tension, and combine to form the number 15, whose "natural" representation in Hebrew letters (*yud-hei*) is another name for God. Moreover, if we count the actual number of letters in this 15-word blessing, we get 60, an echo of the 60 mighty warriors in the previous paragraph! Thus, we can imagine each of the letters of *Birkat Kohanim* as one of those warriors, protecting the *neshamah* and us.[48]

Thus, while the Song of Songs portion of *Hineih Mitato* reminds us of that awesome "terror by night," we derive comfort both from those verses and from *Y'varech'cha*.

XIIIc. *YEILCHU; MI ATAH; V'ATAH*: Verses of final conclusion before closing the aron.

Yeil'chu yonkotav viy'hi chazayit hodo

v're'ach lo kalvanon.

יֵלְכוּ יוֹנְקוֹתָיו וִיהִי כַזַּיִת הוֹדוֹ
וְרֵיחַ לוֹ כַּלְּבָנוֹן.

His boughs shall spread out far; his beauty shall be
like the olive trees, his fragrance like that of Lebanon.

HOSEA 14:7

Mi atah har hagadol lifnei Z'rubavel

l'mishor v'hotzi et ha'even haroshah

t'shu'ot chen chen lah.

מִי אַתָּה הַר הַגָּדוֹל לִפְנֵי זְרֻבָּבֶל
לְמִישֹׁר וְהוֹצִיא אֶת־הָאֶבֶן הָרֹאשָׁה
תְּשֻׁאוֹת חֵן חֵן לָהּ.

Whoever you are, O great mountain in the path
of Zerubavel, turn into level ground! For he shall
produce the excellent stone; it shall be greeted with
shouts of "Beautiful! Beautiful!"

ZECHARIAH 4:7

---

48. Our thanks to Rabbi Jeremy Kalmanofsky for pointing out the symbolic nature of this closing piece of liturgy.

V'atah yigdal na ko'ach Adonai ka'asher dibarta leimor: "V'ulam chai ani v'yimalei ch'vod Adonai et kol ha'aretz."

עַתָּה יִגְדַּל נָא כֹּחַ אֲדֹנָי כַּאֲשֶׁר דִּבַּרְתָּ לֵאמֹר: "וְאוּלָם חַי אָנִי וְיִמָּלֵא כְבוֹד יהוה אֶת כָּל הָאָרֶץ."

Let Adonai's forbearance be great, as You have declared, saying: "as I live, and as Adonai's Presence fills the whole world."

NUMBERS 14:17, 21

COMMENTARY

This sequence includes our third, and final, quotation from the prophet Zechariah. It is a verse particularly suited to conclusions, with its repetition of *chen, chen.*

As we near the end of the ritual, the verses from Numbers offer us a reminder that it's not about us, the *m'taharim,* nor is it about the *neshamah.* Ultimately, it is all about God. "The whole world" is filled with God's glory!

ACTION 2
Recite the closing *Mechilah.*

XIV. *MECHILAH:* We make a closing request for forgiveness from the *met/metah.*

Kavanah: _____ [name of the deceased], we stand here having completed our work. We hope we have treated you with dignity. Please know that we have done our best to prepare you for your final journey.

_____, *ben/bat* [son/daughter of] _____ *v'* [and] _____, we ask your forgiveness for any indignity you may have suffered at the hands of this *Chevra Kadisha,* notwithstanding the loving care and concern that we exercised during

71

this *taharah*. We ask your forgiveness if we did not act according to your honor, even though we acted according to our custom.[49]

COMMENTARY

Placing a version of *Mechilah* here, at the end of the ritual (just before we close the *aron*), allows us to conclude the process in parallel fashion to how we began. We have done the best we can, spiritually and practically. We are reminded that the *neshamah* is still present and aware of what is happening, and we assure him/her that what we have done has not been simply mechanical, but that the full *taharah* ritual has been carried out with the utmost *kavanah*.

ACTION 3

- **Close the *aron*:** Having said our last goodbye to the *met/metah*, we close the *aron*.
- **Place a candle:** Place an unlit *yahrzeit* candle on the foot of the *aron*.

ACTION 4

Recite *Uvinso'a*. This final set of verses is generally recited as the *m'taharim* move the now-closed *aron* out of the *taharah* preparation room to where it will stay until taken to the cemetery (and where *shmirah*—watching of the body—may take place).

XV. UVINSO'A: We move the *met/metah* out of the *taharah* room, and one step closer to eternity.

Kavanah: God, we now ask for assurance from You that this *neshamah* will be protected *for eternity.*

Uvinso'a hamishkan, yoridu oto	וּבִנְסֹעַ הַמִּשְׁכָּן, יוֹרִידוּ אֹתוֹ
hal'vi'im, uvachanot hamishkan, yakimu	הַלְוִיִּם, וּבַחֲנֹת הַמִּשְׁכָּן, יָקִימוּ
oto hal'vi'im, v'hazar hakarev yumat.	אֹתוֹ הַלְוִיִּם, וְהַזָּר הַקָּרֵב יוּמָת.

---

49. Based partly on *PSJC Hevra Kadisha Taharah Manual*

72

When the Tabernacle is to set out, the Levites shall take it down, and when the Tabernacle is to be pitched, the Levites shall set it up; any outsider who encroaches shall be put to death.

NUMBERS 1:51

Vay'hi binso'a ha'aron vayomer Moshe:
"Kumah Adonai v'yafutzu oy'vecha
v'yanusu m'sanecha mipanecha."

וַיְהִי בִּנְסֹעַ הָאָרֹן וַיֹּאמֶר מֹשֶׁה:
"קוּמָה יהוה וְיָפֻצוּ אֹיְבֶיךָ
וְיָנֻסוּ מְשַׂנְאֶיךָ מִפָּנֶיךָ".

When the ark was to set out, Moses would say,
"Advance, Adonai! May Your enemies be scattered,
and may Your foes flee before You!"

NUMBERS 10:35

Lo t'uneh eilecha ra'ah v'nega lo
yikrav b'oholecha: Ki malachav y'tzaveh
lach lishmarcha b'chol d'rachecha: Al
kapayim yisa'uncha pen tigof ba'even
raglecha.

לֹא תְאֻנֶּה אֵלֶיךָ רָעָה וְנֶגַע לֹא
יִקְרַב בְּאָהֳלֶךָ: כִּי מַלְאָכָיו יְצַוֶּה
לָךְ לִשְׁמָרְךָ בְּכָל דְּרָכֶיךָ: עַל
כַּפַּיִם יִשָּׂאוּנְךָ פֶּן תִּגֹּף בָּאֶבֶן
רַגְלֶךָ.

No harm will befall you, no disease touch your tent.
For God will order the angels to guard you wherever
you go. They will carry you in their hands, lest you
hurt your foot on a stone.

PSALMS 91:10-12

Adonai ish milchamah Adonai sh'mo.

יהוה אִישׁ מִלְחָמָה יהוה שְׁמוֹ.

Adonai, the warrior - Adonai is God's name.

EXODUS 15:3

73

Adonai yilachem lachem v'atem

tacharishun.

יהוה יִלָּחֵם לָכֶם וְאַתֶּם
תַּחֲרִשׁוּן.

Adonai will battle for you, you hold your peace.

EXODUS 14:14

COMMENTARY

Each verse in this final set provides further assurance of
protection for the *neshamah* (and, perhaps, for us, the
m'taharim, as well). In the citations from Numbers, we have
both *mishkan* and *aron*. In the desert, one was placed inside
the other, so that within both lay the holy tablets. And both
are, for us, metaphors for the *aron* in which our *met/metah*
now lies. Thus, the invocation of these verses tells us that
the *met/metah* is being compared to those tablets (as it was
likened earlier to a Torah scroll). It is as if any "stranger" who
approaches these "containers" (or approaches our *met/metah*'s
aron) will be put to death. As it (Tabernacle, ark, or casket)
moves forward, God will scatter God's (and the *met/metah*'s)
enemies. Again, the theme of protection is prominent.

Note that Numbers 10:35 is also central to the ritual of
opening the *aron* in the synagogue to take the Torah scroll
out for reading. Upon hearing this verse in the *taharah* ritual,
our minds revert to the pageantry and sacredness, and even
scariness, of that ritual synagogue moment. While moving
(and touching) the *met/metah*'s *aron*, we find ourselves
reenacting those feelings. The antidote to the fear is God's
protection—for the *neshamah* and for us—as expressed in
Numbers.

The verses in Psalms 91:10-12 add angelic protection to that
of God. (Once again, we have the presence of angels.) We,
and the *met/metah*, are assured that "No harm will befall
you." And finally, the verses from Exodus provide us with the
metaphor of God as warrior, "battling" on our behalf.

Could we wish for any greater reassurance than what this
collection of verses provides?

74

In *Ma'avar Yabok*, recitation of these verses seems to be part of the procession to the cemetery, the final physical journey for the body, and a key step in the journey of the *neshamah*. These verses may have made more sense when the *taharah* ritual and the burial were contiguous. Today, with burial usually in a different place from the location of the *taharah* room, and at a somewhat later time than right after *taharah*, the verses may seem a bit redundant. And yet, who is to say when the *met/metah* will be most in need of protection?

ACTION 5
Light the *yahrzeit* candle in silence (with no *brachah*). Exit the room to which the *aron* has been moved, walking backward so as not to turn your back on the *met/metah*.

CHAPTER SUMMARY
By completing this fifth part of the *taharah* ritual, we have done all the necessary tasks that we as part of the Jewish people could do in order to assist the *met/metah* in the final journey.

FINAL COMMENTARY
And so the ritual concludes.

Our focus in these commentaries has been to see how the *taharah* liturgy functions. We have examined the "composed" liturgy as well as the Biblical and Rabbinic citations to see:
* what the quoted passages meant in their original settings;
* what purposes the various components of the liturgy serve in their *taharah* setting;
* how echoes of the liturgy from other settings enhance their meaning; and
* how the liturgy responds to the needs of each of the "entities" in the room, especially the emotions—fears and hopes—that might be in the minds of the *m'taharim*.

We know that each time we perform this *mitzvah*, none of us emerges from the *taharah* room exactly the same as when we entered. We hope that our examination of the liturgy will illuminate and intensify its meaning for the *m'taharim,* so that we are able to provide genuine *k'vod hamet,* serving the *metim* with the greatest possible *kavanah,* and enriching our own experience.

Chapter 10
Following the Ritual

Just as the *taharah* ritual itself was preceded by preparatory activities, first outside the *taharah* room and then inside the room, so, symmetrically, the ritual is concluded by follow-up activities, first inside the *taharah* room and then outside.

INSIDE THE *TAHARAH* ROOM

The *m'taharim* have now completed the main portion of *taharah*. The tasks that remain include cleaning the *taharah* room and washing hands.

✎ Clean the *taharah* room

After removing the *met/metah* from the room, the *m'taharim* should return to clean the *taharah* tools and throw away any used items. Remove gloves and gowns, and place any gowns or materials that need to be washed in a separate bag.

✎ Do a supply inventory

The *rosh* (team leader) should do an inventory of the *taharah* supplies, and restock the supply box to the extent possible. The *rosh* should contact the *Chevra Kadisha* chair with information about replenishing the supplies.

OUTSIDE THE *TAHARAH* ROOM

What remains for the *m'taharim* is to wash hands and, if they choose, conduct a closing ceremony for themselves. If feasible, these activities might take place outside the funeral home itself.

✎ Wash hands

Having removed and discarded their gloves inside the *taharah* room, the *m'taharim* should wash their hands outside the *taharah* room. As before, they wash each of their hands three times, alternating between the right and left hand and beginning with the right one. Use a hand-washing cup or other vessel to pour the water, do not recite a *brachah*, and allow hands to air dry.

✎ Optional closing ceremony

The *m'taharim* may choose to participate in the following closing ceremony, using some or all of the texts below. As with the optional prayer before *taharah,* these closing prayers might be read by individuals, read responsively, or read in unison.

The eyes of all look to You expectantly,
  and You give them their food when it is due.

PSALMS 145:15

☙

A person may plot out a course,
  but it is Adonai who directs one's steps.

PROVERBS 16:9

☙

Indeed, one does not know what it is to happen; even when it is on the point of happening, who can tell that person?

ECCLESIASTES 8:7

☙

What, then, can I count on, Adonai?
  In You my hope lies.

PSALMS 39:8

☙

We set our hope on Adonai,
  God is our help and shield.

PSALMS 33:20

☙

I look to Adonai;
  I look to God;
  I await God's word.
I am more eager for Adonai
    than watchmen for the morning,
    watchmen for the morning.

PSALMS 130:5-6

☙

I long for Your deliverance;
  I hope for Your word.

My eyes pine away for Your promise;
I say, "When will You comfort me?"

PSALMS 119:81-82

My eyes are ever toward Adonai,
For God will loose my feet from the net.
Turn to me, have mercy on me,
for I am alone and afflicted.

PSALMS 25:15-16

My eyes are ever toward Adonai,

Safe and sound, I lie down and sleep,
For You alone, O God, keep me secure.

PSALMS 4:9

You have made *Adam* little less than divine,
and adorned *Adam* with glory and majesty;
You have made *Adam* ruler over Your handiwork,
Laying the world at *Adam's* feet.

PSALMS 8:6-7

O Adonai, our God,
how majestic is Your name throughout the earth.
What is *Adam* that You have been mindful of him (us)
Mortal being that You have taken note of him (us).

PSALMS 8:2, 5

GROUP SHARING

Some *Chevra Kadisha* groups choose to spend a few minutes sharing responses to the experience of the *taharah* they have just performed together. This can include a range of areas, such as emotions that have arisen during the ritual and ideas about how to improve the working practice of the *Chevra*.

FINAL GROUP PRAYER

As a final collective prayer, the *m'taharim* might recite the following:

Creator of the universe, we have just completed our act of *g'milut chesed* for _____ [name of the deceased].

We thank you for the strength and courage to perform this *mitzvah*. We appreciate participating in this *Chevra Kadisha*, this sacred fellowship, and cherish the bond that brings us together.

Team members may then observe a moment of silence for private meditation and reflection.

Appendix 1
Glossary of Hebrew Terms*

afar	dust, dirt, soil; for *taharah*, *afar* comes from Israel
alef, bet, gimel, dalet	the first four letters of the Hebrew alphabet, used to count the twists when tying *tachrichim* knots
Amidah	"Standing prayer"—the core of the daily prayer services
aron	casket
avi avot hatumah	lit. "father of fathers of *tumah*," i.e., the ultimate source of *tumah*; touching a dead body is the highest form of *tumah*
avnet	belt—part of *tachrichim*
avodat hakodesh	holy work
Birkat Kohanim	Priestly blessing (also referred to as *Y'varech'cha*, from the first word of the blessing)
brachah	blessing
brit	covenant; specifically, the covenant of circumcision
chesed shel emet	lit. "kindness of truth"—the highest act of kindness
Chevra Kadisha	lit. "Holy Society"—the group responsible for all matters pertaining to the dead
Gehenna	the netherworld
gemilut chesed	acts of kindness
halanah	placing the *met/metah* in the *aron*—part of *taharah* ritual
halbashah	dressing the *met/metah*—part of *taharah* ritual
Kabbalah	the texts from the mystical tradition in Judaism; also, more broadly, that tradition itself

*Some words are difficult to translate. We have made an effort to explain the terms as they apply to the ritual of *taharah*.

kavanah (pl. *kavanot*)	intention; also used to refer to introductions to prayers
kedushah	sanctity
kippah	head covering (*yarmulke* in Yiddish)
kittel	outer jacket—part of *tachrichim*; also worn by one or both of those getting married and on Yom Kippur and Pesach
kohen (pl. *kohanim*)	priest; those descended from the priests
Kohen Gadol	High Priest
k'tonet	shirt or blouse—part of *tachrichim*
k'vod	respect
k'vod hamet	respect for the deceased
Magen David	Star of David
m'chayei hametim	resurrection of the dead
mechilah	forgiveness; also (cap.), a prayer asking forgiveness
met/metah/metim (m., f., pl.)	deceased person
michnasayim	trousers—part of *tachrichim*
midrash	commentary
mikveh	pool of water, reservoir sometimes used in a *taharah* (as well as for other ritual cleansing)
mishkan	Temple or tabernacle
mitznefet	head covering – part of *tachrichim*
mitzvah (pl. *mitzvot*)	commandment in Jewish law
m'taharim	those performing the *taharah*
nechamah	comfort
neshamah	soul
nichum aveilim	comforting the mourners
Rabban Gamliel	3rd century rabbi whose rulings addressed equality, simplicity, and low prices in issues related to funeral and burial; his rulings became the foundation of Jewish practice
rechitzah	washing – part of *taharah* ritual
rosh	the head of the group of *m'taharim*
sheva brachot	the seven blessings offered to the bride and groom
shmirah	guarding, watching
sovev	sheet that wraps the body in the *aron*
tachrichim	burial garments

taharah	purification or purity; refers to the entire procedure and prayers when preparing bodies for burial, as well as to certain elements of that procedure; also refers to ritual purification with water in other contexts
tahor/t'horah (m., f.)	pure (but see discussion in Chapter 1)
tallit	prayer shawl
tamei/tumah	impure/impurity (but see discussion in Chapter 1)
tzedakah	lit. "righteousness"; used to refer to the obligation to give funds for the care of the needy
yahrzeit	anniversary of a person's death
z'chut avot	lit. "merits of the ancestors"; refers to the concepts that one gains something as a result of relationship with the ancestors
Zechariah	Prophet who wrote about the return to Zion after the Babylonian exile and the role of the *Kohen Gadol*

Appendix 2
Chevra Kadisha **Leader's Report Form**

Date: _____   Time started: _____

Place: _____   Time ended: _____

English name of *met/metah*: _____

Hebrew name of *met/metah*: _____

Team leader: _____

Team members: _____

Complications: _____

_____

Please list any jewelry and/or other items that were removed from the

met/metah and report where they were put:_____

_____

_____

List any questions asked about *taharah* and who was asked:_____

_____

Explain any problems encountered during *taharah*:_____

_____

_____

Suggestions: _____

Signed _____ , Team leader

Appendix 3
Supplies for *Taharah*

Supply List
You will need the following supplies to perform *taharah*. Most of these items should be kept in a supply box at the synagogue, temple, or funeral home. We also recommend that every *Chevra Kadisha* maintain reserve supplies of these items.

For team members
-washable gowns

-surgical gloves

-disposable masks

-goggles

-disposable shoe covers

For washing
-four varnished wooden two-by-fours

-a cup for washing hands

-three buckets

-wooden nail cleaners

-nail polish remover

-cotton balls

-washcloths or disposable towels

-towels or sheets for drying

-sheets for covering the body during cleaning

-large bandages

-adult diapers

-surgical tape

For dressing
-a tallit, preferably one that belonged to the *met/metah*

-*kippot*

-*afar* (soil) from Israel

-pottery shards

-*tachrichim* (shrouds)

Miscellaneous
-*aron* (casket)

-*Magen David* and wood glue

-*yahrzeit* candles and matches

-enlarged copies of Hebrew prayers

-freestanding easel

Appendix 4
Knots[50]

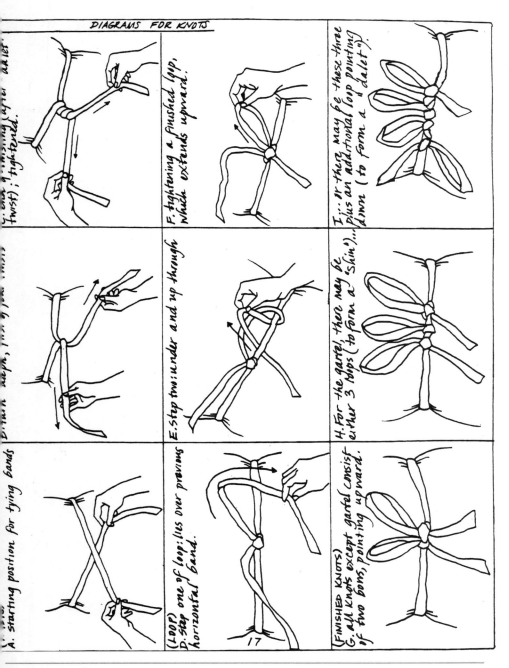

DIAGRAMS FOR KNOTS

A. starting position for tying bands

(LOOP)
D. Step one of loop: lies over previous horizontal band.

E. Step two: under and up through

F. tightening a finished loop, which extends upward.

G. all knots except gartel consist of two bows, pointing upward.
(FINISHED KNOTS)

H. For the gartel, there may be either 3 loops (to form a "shin")...

I. ...or there may be these three plus an additional loop pointing down (to form a "dalet").

17

50. Schlingenbaum, p. 17.

Bibliography

Bayliss, Joan, Irwin Noparstak, and Jesse Rappaport. *Revised Tahara Manual*. Eugene, OR: Temple Beth Israel, 2000.

Berakhiah, Rabbi Aharon, of Modena. *Ma'avar Yabok* (1626). Jerusalem: Ahavat Shalom, Critical edition 5756 (Hebrew).

Berman, Rochel. *Dignity Beyond Death: The Jewish Preparation for Burial*. Jerusalem/New York: Urim Publications, 2005.

Epstein, Rabbi Mosha. *Tahara Manual of Practices*, Third Edition. Bridgeport, CT: 2005.

Golinkin, Rabbi David. *The Taharah Ritual*. Jerusalem: The Va'ad Halacha of the Rabbinical Assembly of Israel, V. 5. 5752-5754.

Goodman, Rabbi Arnold. *A Plain Pine Box, Augmented Edition*. New York, NY: Ktav, 2003.

Greenhough, Lynn. *Handbook for Hevra Kadisha Members*. 2008.

Guide to Taharah Practices, For Men. Chevy Chase, MD: Ohr Kodesh Congregation Funeral Practices Committee, 2002.

Kavod v'Nichum—Jewish Funerals, Burial and Mourning (North American organization providing education and resources on *Chevra Kadisha*). www.jewish-funerals.org

Lamm, Maurice. *The Jewish Way in Death and Mourning*. NY: Jonathan David, 1969.

Lieberman, Lynn. *Procedures for the Chevra Kadisha*. Melbourne, FL: 1994.

Light, Rick. *Guidelines for Performing Tahara*. Prepared for the Chevra Kadisha of Northern New Mexico, Second Edition. Los Alamos, NM: Los Alamos Jewish Center, 2005.

Liturgy for Taharah. Philadelphia: Reconstructionist Hevrah Kadishah of Philadelphia, n.d.

Milgrom, Jo. *A Selection of Verses for the Chevra Kadisha*. Berkeley, CA: Unpublished manuscript.

Moss, Steven. "The Attitude Toward Sickness, Dying and Death as Expressed in the Liturgical Works *Maavor Yabok* and *Sefer Hahayiim*." MA Thesis, Hebrew Union College-Jewish Institute of Religion, 1974.

PSJC Hevra Kadisha Taharah Manual, 2nd ed. Brooklyn, NY: Park Slope Jewish Center, 2009.

Reconstructionist Tahara Handbook for Women and Men. Bethesda, MD: Adat Shalom Chevra Kadisha, 2005.

Regulations and Procedure including Traditional Prayers and Translations for the Jewish Sacred Society. Chicago, IL: Jewish Sacred Society, n.d.

Ridberg, Rabbi Yael, et al. *Tahara Manual for B'nai Jeshurun*. New York, NY: Hevra Kadisha of B'nai Jeshurin, 5760.

Scherman, Rabbi Nosson, trans. and Rabbi Meir Zlotowitz, ed. *The Complete ArtScroll Siddur*, Brooklyn: Mesorah Publications, Ltd. 1984.

Schlingenbaum, Yechezkel. *Tahara Guide Prepared for the New Haven Chevra Kadisha*. New Haven, CT: 1993.

Schorr, Rabbi Yisroel Simcha, et al., *Talmud Bavli, ArtScroll Series/ Schottenstein Edition*. Brooklyn, NY: Mesorah Publications, Ltd.

Taharah Guide for Men's and Women's Chevra Kadisha. New York, NY: Congregation Kehilath Jeshurun, n.d.

Tanakh: A New Translation of the Holy Scriptures According to the Traditional Hebrew Text. Jewish Publication Society, Philadelphia, NY, Jerusalem: 1985.

Tucazinsky, Yechiel Michel. *Gesher Hachayim* (The Bridge of Life). Second edition. Jerusalem: 1960 (English edition, 1983 – Part 3 only).

THE GAMLIEL INSTITUTE is a center for study, training, and advocacy concerning Jewish end of life practices where leaders are educated and trained to create a holistic end-of-life care continuum for their local communities. The Gamliel Institute strives to instill in its leaders a driving passion to recapture the mitzvah of *Chevra Kadisha* by ensuring that that future leaders' Jewish knowledge is deeper and their experiences more emotional, transformative, and spiritual. The Institute is a project of Kavod V'Nichum (Honor and Comfort), a North American organization which provides assistance, training, and resources about Jewish death and bereavement practice for *Chevra Kadisha* groups and bereavement committees in synagogues and communities throughout the U.S. and Canada.

SINAI MEMORIAL CHAPEL CHEVRA KADISHA continually strives to be the pre-eminent provider of Jewish funeral and burial services to the entire Jewish community of the San Francisco Bay Area. As an essential community service organization, we are committed to maintaining both our sacred and not-for-profit traditions, while embracing evolving Jewish practices. Our hallmarks will always be *Chesed Shel Emet* and *Kavod Hamet*, to honor the dignity of the deceased, and to provide compassion and support for the living. We are committed to excellence in all we do: delivering unrivaled services, knowledgeable staff, comforting facilities, honesty and integrity in all of our practices, and fair prices.

Also available from EKS Publishing:

Give Me Your Hand:
Traditional and Practical Guidance on Visiting the Sick

K'vod Hamet: A Guide for the Bereaved

Contact EKS for a free catalog
877-7-HEBREW (877-743-2739)
orders@ekspublishing.com